Nicholson's

Visitor's London

When you're a visitor in a strange city you expect to be able to buy a good guide book — one that is accurate, concise and describes everything you could possibly want to see, do and enjoy during your stay.

Well, here it is — Visitor's London one of the popular range of Nicholson's London guides. Based on Nicholson's long experience of what visitors to London want to know, the following pages are packed with information on every conceivable London topic from airports to zoos. You can get to know and love this city with Visitor's London — it's pocket size too.

D1142533

London Map
© Robert Nicholson Publications Limited based upon the Ordnance Survey map with the sanction of the Controller of Her Majesty's Stationery Office, Crown Copyright reserved.

© Robert Nicholson Publications Limited
24 Highbury Crescent, London N5 1RX

ISBN 0 905522 21 4

UR-2/78-50-lu77.

ROBERT NICHOLSON PUBLICATIONS
COMMUNICA-EUROPA

Contents

SHOPPING 70

London is a marvellous shopping centre. There are so many wonderful shops that it's difficult to get to them all. For this reason you'll find the shop by shop street maps, hints on what to buy, details of tax concessions and the clothes and measure conversion charts, extremely useful.

GETTING OUT 82

It's a great city, but there are also many beautiful and exciting places outside London – historic towns and lordly country houses, all within easy reach. In this section you'll also find all the means of transport out of London, including airports and car ferries for those who are travelling even further afield.

INFORMATION 91

Everything you need to know to keep you going – banks and foreign exchange, tourist offices, telephone services, where you can get travel information, book tours, hire cars or taxis, find out about daily events – even how to get hold of emergency services. Relax. You've got London in your pocket.

L	lunch
D	dinner
B	buffet

Average prices for a meal without wine:

£	Under £4.00 per person
££	Under £8.00 per person
£££	Over £8.00 per person
Children	Children welcome, sometimes with a reduction in price.
Reserve	It is advisable to reserve
A	Access Cards accepted
Ax	American Express
B	Barclay Card
Cb	Carte Blanche
Dc	Diners Club
E	Eurocard
M	Membership necessary

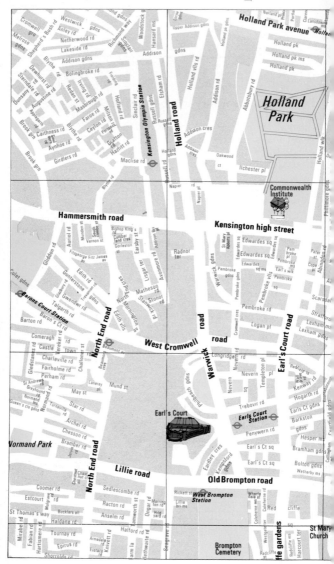

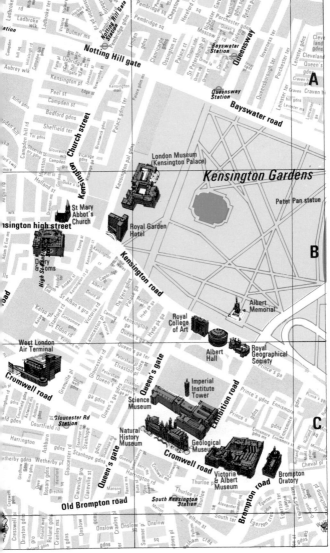

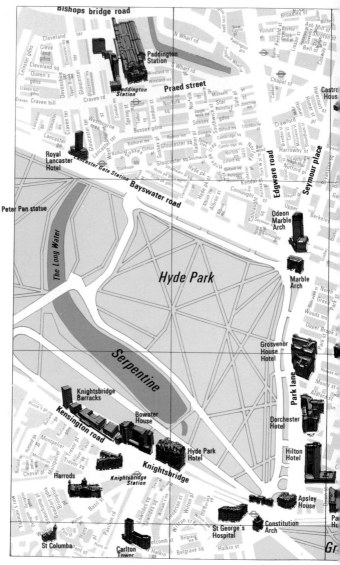

Taunton pl
Park road
Sussex
Melbury
Boston st
Balcombe st
Ivor pl
Taunton ms
Dorset
Clarence ga
Melcombe pl
sq
Dorset
Clarence ter
Gloucester pl
Glentworth st
Chagford st
Cornwall ter
York
Bickenhall st
Alsop pl
Melcombe st
Crawford st
Baker street
Baker St Station
Planetarium

Bedford College

Regents Park

Outer circle

A

Albany street

Outer circle

Cambridge Gate

Chester

Munster sq

Chiltern st
Madame Tussauds
Marylebone road
York ter
Upper Harley
Harley
Park sq W
Park sq E
St. Mary Magdalene

York st
Gloucester
Montagu
Dorset
Paddington st
Nottingham st
Marylebone high st
Devonshire st
Weymouth st
Park cres
Regents Park Station
Gt Portland St Station
Euston road
Warren st
Warren St St

Baker street
Blandford st
Manchester st
Chiltern st
Moxon st
Aybrook st
Cramer st
Luxborough st
Marylebone
New Cavendish st
Royal Institute of British Architects
Greenwell
Carburton
Warren

Wallace Collection
Portman
Fitzhardinge
Manchester
Thayer st
Hinde st
Bentinck st
Marylebone la
Bulstrode st
Welbeck st
New Cavendish st
Weymouth st
Hallam st
Cavendish
Hallam st
Clipstone st
Cleveland st
G.P.O. Tower

B

Whitfield st
Howland st
Goodge St Station

Selfridges
Wigmore street
Welbeck st
Wimpole st
Henrietta pl
Marg
Little Portland
Langham
Riding House st
Hanson st
Cleveland st

Oxford street
Duke st
Gilbert st
Binney st
Weighhouse
Davies st
Barrett st
Bond St Station
James st
Stratford pl
Marylebone la
Welbeck st
Wimpole st
Cavendish
Margaret
Broadcasting House
Great Titchfield st
Little Titchfield st
Gt Portland st
All Saints
Mortimer street
Nassau st
Eastcastle st
Berners st
Newman st
Middlesex Hospital
Fort st
Riding House
Tottenham
Scala
Goodge st
Chitty st
Goodge street

Charlotte

U.S.A. Embassy
Grosvenor sq
Brook st
Three Kings yd
Carlos pl
Gilbert st
George
Grosvenor sq
Claridges Hotel
St George's
Hanover sq
Princes
Pollen
Oxford Circus Station
Ramillies st
Argyle st
Great Marlborough st
Noel
Poland st
D'arblay
Oxford street
Wardour st
Soho
Windmill st
Percy st
Rathbone
Stephen
Tudor pl

C

Connaught Hotel
Mount
Davies st
Bourdon st
Grosvenor hill
New Bond Street
Maddox st
Conduit st
St George's
Gt Marlborough st
Fouberts pl
Kingly st
Ganton st
Marshall st
Carnaby st
Broadwick st
Berwick st
Wardour st
Dean st
Carlisle
St Anne's ct
Soho

Grosvenor Chapel
Farm st
Mount
Reeves ms
Berkeley sq
Berkeley st
Bruton pl
Bruton st
Bruton la
Barlow
Grafton
Boyle st
New Burlington st
Clifford st
Cork st
Savile row
Vigo st
Warwick st
Beak st
Upper John st
Lower John st
Golden sq
Brewer st
Peter st
Meard
Dean st
Rupert st
Greek st
Compton st
St Anne's

Royal Academy
Hill
Hay's ms
Chesterfield
Charles st
Curzon st
Queen st
Bolton st
Clarges st
Clarges ms
Berkeley
Hay Hill
Dover st
Albemarle st
Old Bond st
Stafford st
Bennet st
St James's
St James's
Regent
Sherwood
Denman st
Brewer st
Glasshouse st
Rupert st
Archer st
Wardour st
Shaftesbury
St John's Hospital
Coventry st
Panton st
St James's

Green Park Station
White Horse st
Half Moon st
Shepherd
Down st
Brick st
Park la
Piccadilly
Ritz Hotel
Arlington st
Park pl
St James's pl
Queen's walk
St James's st
King st
Economist Building
St James's sq
Charles II st
Lower Regent
Whitcomb st
Leicester Sq Station
Leicester sq
Orange st
Irving st
Cranbourn st
Covent G
Sta

Charing Cross road
Cambridge
Earl
Lichfield
Litchfield
Garrick st
Cecil ct
St Martin's la

n Park

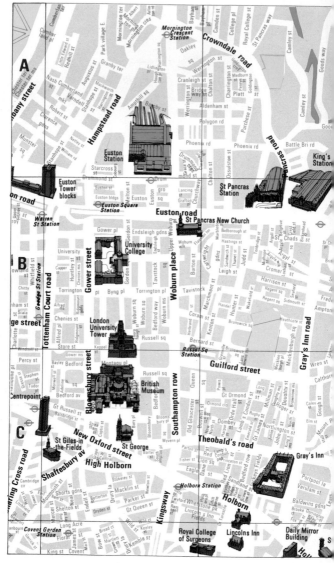

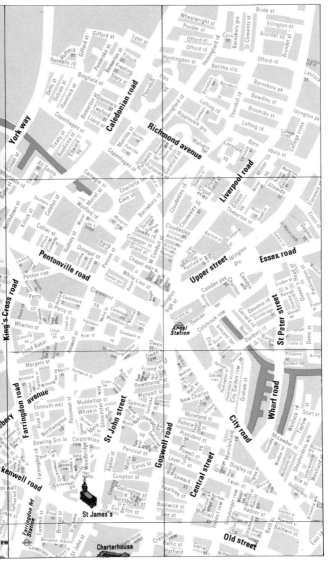

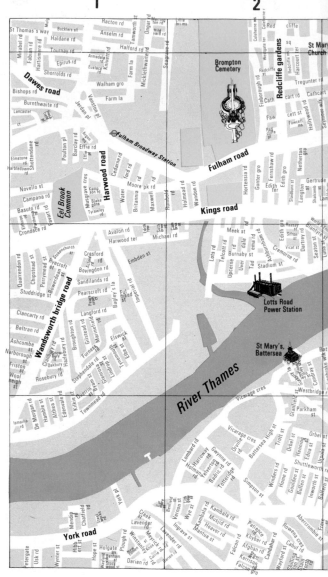

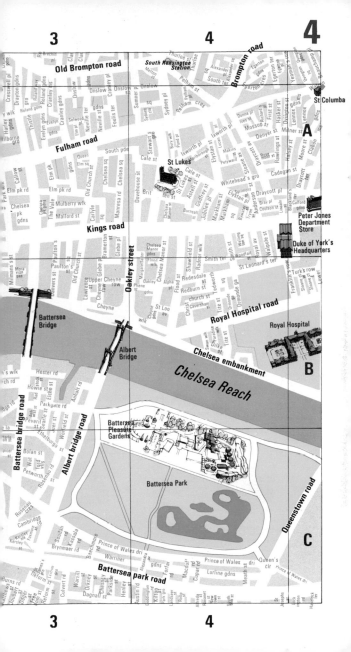

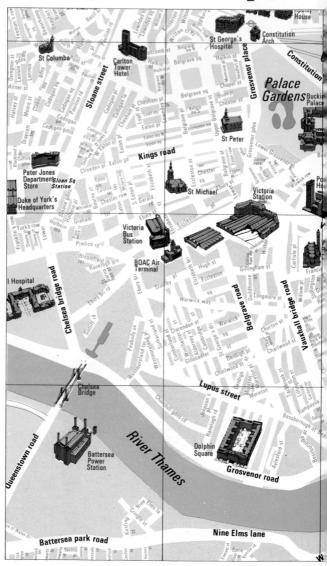

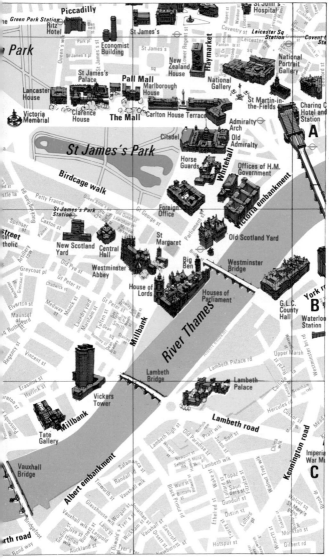

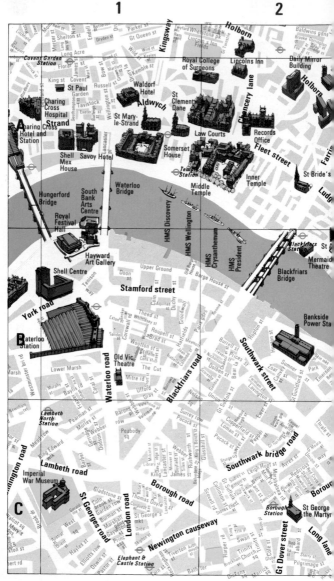

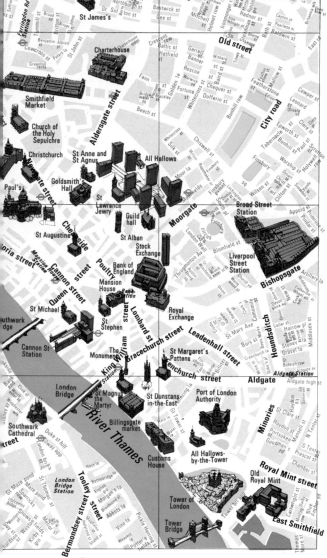

Map Index

HISTORIC LONDON

Historic buildings

This list cover the most important of the historic houses, notable buildings, monuments, characteristic streets and districts, and items of general historic interest. Look also under sections such as 'Churches' or 'Parks'.

Bank of England
Threadneedle St EC2. 01-601 4444. The vaults hold the nation's gold reserves. Outer walls are still the original design by Sir John Soane, architect to the Bank from 1788-1833. Rebuilt by Sir H. Baker 1925-33.

Buckingham Palace
St James's Park SW1. 01-930 4832. The permanent London palace of the reigning Sovereign. Originally built 1705; remodelled by Nash 1825; refaced 1913 by Sir Aston Webb.

Burlington Arcade
Piccadilly W1. 1819 Regency shopping promenade with original shop windows. Still employs a beadle to preserve the gracious atmosphere.

Burlington House
Piccadilly W1. Victorian-Renaissance façade on one of the great 18th cent palaces. Houses the Royal Academy and various Royal Societies.

Charing Cross WC2
The Charing Cross was the last of the stone crosses set up by Edward I to mark the funeral resting places of Queen Eleanor's body on its way to Westminster Abbey. Originally placed where Trafalgar Square now is, it was demolished in 1647 and the statue of Charles I now stands in its place. The stone cross in the station courtyard is a replica.

Chelsea Royal Hospital
Chelsea embankment SW3. A hospital for old soldiers. Fine, austere building. 1682 by Wren. Stables 1814 by Sir John Soane. Museum *OPEN 10.00-12.00 & 14.00-16.30 Mon-Sat, 14.00-16.30 Sun. CLOSED G. Fri, Easter Sun, Xmas. Free.*

Chiswick House
Burlington Lane W4. 01-994 3299. Lovely Palladian villa built in the grand manner by 3rd Earl of Burlington 1725-

30. Fine interiors and gardens by William Kent. *OPEN 09.30-13.00, 14.00-16.00; until 17.30 Mar, Apr & Oct; until 19.00 May-Sept. CLOSED Mon, Tues Oct-Mar, Xmas Eve, Xmas, Box. Small admission charge.*

Clarence House
Stable Yard Gate SW1. Mansion by Nash 1825. Now the home of the Queen Mother.

College of Arms
Queen Victoria St EC4. 01-248 2762. Handsome late 17th cent building which houses the official records of English and Welsh heraldry and genealogy.

Fenton House
Hampstead Grove NW3. 01-435 3471. Built in 1693. Collection of early keyboard instruments and porcelain. Gardens. *OPEN 11.00-17.00 Wed-Sat, 14.00-17.00 Sun. CLOSED G. Fri, Xmas. Admission charge.*

Gray's Inn
Holborn WC1. 01-242 8591. Entrance from passage next to 22 High Holborn. An Inn of Court since 14th cent. The Hall (16th cent) and 'Buildings' restored after bomb damage. Gardens were laid out by Francis Bacon. *Hall OPEN by written application to the Under Treasurer. Gardens OPEN Jun-Jul 12.00-14.00; Aug 08.00-18.00. CLOSED Sat, Sun, B. Hols. Free.*

Greenwich
Six miles downriver and associated with England's former sea power. The following are notable:

Greenwich: Charlton House
Charlton Rd SE7. 01-856 3951. Perfect small red brick Jacobean manor house on an 'H' plan, built 1607-12. Fine ceilings, staircase and some bizarre chimney-pieces. *OPEN by appointment only. Contact warden.*

Greenwich: The Queen's House
Romney Rd SE10. 01-858 4422. Now part of the National Maritime Museum. Built by Inigo Jones 1619 for the Queen of Denmark. *OPEN 10.00-18.00 Mon-Sat, 14.30-1800 Sun in summer; 10.00-17.00 winter. CLOSED G. Fri, Xmas, Box, New Year's. Free.*

Greenwich: Royal Hospital
Greenwich SE10. 01-858 2154. Now the Royal Naval

College, the site of the former Royal palace for the Tudor Sovereigns. A fine and interesting group of classical buildings by Webb 1664, Wren 1692 and Vanbrugh 1728. Chapel by James 'Athenian' Stuart 1789 and Painted Hall by Thornhill. *OPEN 14.30-17.00. CLOSED Thur. Free.*

Greenwich: Rotunda Museum
Woolwich Common SE18. Pavilion by Nash 1814. Little known museum full of guns of the Royal Artillery. *OPEN 10.00-12.45 & 14.00-17.00. Winter 16.00 (Sun 14.00-17.00). Free.*

Greenwich: Old Royal Observatory
Greenwich Park SE10. 01-858 4422. Formerly the Greenwich Observatory. Part of the National Maritime Museum and includes Flamsteed House. Designed by Wren and founded by Charles II in 1675. Time and astronomical instruments. *OPEN 10.00-18.00, Winter 17.00 (Sun 14.30-18.00, Winter 17.00.) CLOSED G. Fri, Xmas Eve, Xmas & Box.* also a Planetarium: phone for times of showing.

Guildhall
Off Gresham St EC2. 01-606 3030. 15th cent with facade by George Dance 1789 and later restorations by Sir Giles Gilbert Scott. The Great Hall is used for ceremonial occasions. Medieval groined vaulting in crypts. Library, Art Gallery, museum of clocks and watches. *Great Hall OPEN 10.00-17.00 Mon-Sat, 14.00-17.00 Sun, May-Sept & B. Hols. CLOSED New Year's, G. Fri, Xmas, Box. Free. Exhibition Hall OPEN 10.00-17.00 Mon-Fri, Wed until 19.00 CLOSED B. Hols. Free. Art Gallery OPEN 10.00-17.00 Mon-Sat. CLOSED B. Hols. Usually free.*

Henry VIII's Wine Cellar
Whitehall SW1. Genuine Tudor wine cellar built for Cardinal Wolsey. All that remains of Tudor Whitehall Palace. *OPEN Sat afternoons by pass from the Dept of the Environment, Room 4/58, Elizabeth House, York Rd SE1.*

Highgate Cemetery
Swains Lane N6. Spookiest place in London. Egyptian catacombs reveal coffins within open tombs. Karl Marx's tomb. *OPEN 09.00-16.30 Mon-Sat, 14.00-16.00 Sun. Free.*

Houses of Parliament
St Margaret St SW1. 01-219 3000. Victorian-Gothic building 1840-68 by Sir Charles Barry and A. W. N. Pugin. Westminster Hall was built in 1099 as the Great Hall of William Rufus' new palace; the roof dates from the late 14th cent. House of Lords admission at St Stephen's entrance (Old Palace Yard side) or by Westminster Hall if wet. House of Commons admission

only by permission from MP or by queueing outside St Stephen's entrance on day of debate. Tour of Parliament admission at Sovereign's Entrance, House of Lords. *When neither House is sitting OPEN 10.00-16.30 Sat, Easter Mon & Tues; Spring hol Mon & Tues; Aug Mon, Tues & Thur; Sept Thur. Conducted tours Sat. During sessions queue admitted from 16.15 Mon-Thur, 11.30 Fri to House of Commons, and from 14.40 Mon-Wed, 15.10 Thur to House of Lords. Westminster Hall OPEN when Parliament is in session but neither House is sitting, 10.00-13.00 Mon-Thur, 10.00-17.00 Sat. During recess 10.00-16.00 Mon-Fri, 10.00-17.00 Sat. CLOSED G. Fri, Xmas, Box.* All free.

Kensington Palace
Kensington Gardens W8. Simple and charming building acquired by William III in 1689 as a palace. Exterior altered by Wren, interior by William Kent. Queen Victoria and Queen Mary born here. The warm brick Orangery was built 1704 by Hawksmoor. State apartments *OPEN Mar-Sept 10.00-18.00 Mon-Sat, 14.00-18.00 Sun; Oct 10.00-17.00 Mon-Sat, 14.00-17.00 Sun; Nov-Feb 10.00-16.00 Mon-Sat, 14.00-16.00 Sun. CLOSED G. Fri, Xmas, Box, New Year's.*

Lambeth Palace
Lambeth Palace Rd SE1. 01-928 6222 (Library only). The London residence of the Archbishop of Canterbury. 15th cent. Fine medieval crypt and 17th cent hall. Portraits from 16th-19th cent. Library for readers only, *OPEN 10.00-17.00 Mon-Fri. CLOSED at conference times, Easter, B. Hols and Xmas.*

Law Courts
Strand WC2. 01-405 7641. Massive Victorian-Gothic building, housing the Royal Courts of Justice. *OPEN to public 10.00-16.30 Mon-Fri. CLOSED Aug and Sept.*

Leadenhall Market
Gracechurch St EC3. Impressive Victorian glass and iron hall 1881, housing the poultry market.

Lincoln's Inn

Lincoln's Inn WC2. 01-405 1393. An Inn of Court. 17th cent. New Square, gardens, barristers' chambers and solicitors' offices. A chapel by Inigo Jones (1623) and the 15th cent Old Hall. Great Hall was built in 1845. The 'Stone Buildings' are by Sir Robert Taylor and were begun in 1774. Still has Dickens atmosphere. *Apply to Gatehouse in Chancery Lane for admission to Hall and Chapel. Mon-Fri. Free.*

Lincoln's Inn Fields WC2

7 acres of gardens laid out by Inigo Jones 1618. Once a famous duelling ground. Nos. 12-14 built 1792 by Sir John Soane. Nos. 57-8 built 1730 by Henry Joynes. Nos. 59 & 60 built 1640 by Inigo Jones. *OPEN Tues-Sat 10.00-17.00. CLOSED Sun, Mon & B. Hols.*

London's Wall

Surviving parts of the medieval wall around the old city of London can still be seen at St Alphage on the north side of London Wall EC1; St Giles churchyard; Cripplegate EC1; Jewry St EC3; off Trinity Square EC3 and in the Tower of London.

Mansion House

Opposite Bank of England EC2. 01-626 2500. Official residence of the Lord Mayor. Palladian building by George Dance 1739. Completed 1752. *OPEN alternate Sat mornings by appointment.* Parties limited to 30.

Marlborough House

Marlborough Gate, Pall Mall SW1. 01-839 3411. Designed by Wren 1710. Contains a painted ceiling by Genti Peschi which was originally designed for the Queen's House at Greenwich. The simple classical-style Queen's Chapel in the grounds is by Inigo Jones, 1626. *Not open to the public.*

Old Bailey

Old Bailey EC4. 01-248 3277. The Central Criminal Court. On the site of old Newgate Prison. *Trials open to the public. Gallery OPEN 10.30-13.00 & 14.00-16.00 Mon-Fri. Minimum age 14. Free.*

Old Curiosity Shop

13-14 Portsmouth St WC2. 01-405 9891. Tudor house built 1567 and now an antique shop. Immortalised by Dickens in 'The Old Curiosity Shop'. *OPEN daily Apr-Oct 09.00-17.30; Nov-Mar 09.30-17.30. Free.*

Old Palace

Old Palace Rd, Croydon, Surrey. 01-688 2027. Seat of the Archbishop of Canterbury for 1,000 years. Tudor chapel. *OPEN various afternoons during the year, 14.00-17.30. Conducted tours. Phone for details. Admission charge.*

Prince Henry's Rooms
17 Fleet St EC4. 01-353 7323. From 1610; oldest domestic building in London. Named after the son of James I. Fine plaster ceiling and carved oak panelling. *OPEN 13.45-17.00 Mon-Fri, 13.45-16.30 Sat. Free.*

Roman Bath
5 Strand Lane WC2. Disputed origin: restored in the 17th cent. *OPEN 10.00-12.30 Mon-Sat. CLOSED Sun, G. Fri, Xmas. Small admission charge.*

Royal Exchange
Corner of Threadneedle St and Cornhill EC3. Built in 1884 by Tite. The third building on this site. Originally founded as a market for merchants and craftsmen in 1564, and destroyed in the Great Fire. The second building was also burnt down in 1838. Ambulatory containing statues and mural painting and courtyard. *OPEN 10.00-16.00 Mon-Fri, 10.00-12.00 Sat. CLOSED Sun & B. Hols.*

Royal Mews
Buckingham Palace Rd SW1. The Queen's horses and carriages, including the Coronation coach. *OPEN 14.00-16.00 Wed & Thur. CLOSED Royal Ascot week. Admission charge.*

Royal Opera Arcade
Between Pall Mall and Charles II St SW1. John Nash 1816, London's earliest arcade. Pure Regency; bow-fronted shops, glass domed vaults and elegant lamps.

St James's Palace
Pall Mall SW1. Built by Henry VIII with many later additions. Still officially a Royal residence. Ceiling of Chapel Royal by Holbein. *No admission to palace. Entry to courtyards only.*

Skinners Hall
8 Dowgate Hill EC4. 01-236 5629. 17th-18th cent buildings and quiet arcaded courtyard.

Somerset House
Strand WC2. On the site of an unfinished 16th cent palace. By Sir W. Chambers 1776. Used to house the

register of births, marriages and deaths in England and Wales, now holds the Registry of divorce, wills and probate and the Inland Revenue.

Stock Exchange

Old Broad St EC2. 01-588 2355. Entrance to public gallery at corner of Threadneedle St and Old Broad St, showing the turmoil of 2,000 soberly dressed members milling below. Films shown in adjoining cinema. *Gallery OPEN 10.00-15.15 Mon-Fri. Last tour begins 14.30. CLOSED G. Fri, B. Hols, Xmas, New Year's. Free.* Parties up to 40, ring or write to P.R. Dept.

The Temple

Inner Temple, Crown Office Row EC4. 01-353 4355. Middle Temple, Middle Temple Lane EC4. 01-353 4355. Both are Inns of Court. Enter by Wren's gatehouse, 1685, in Middle Temple Lane. An extensive area of courtyards, alleys, gardens and warm brick buildings. Middle Hall 1570. The Temple Church is an early Gothic 'round church' built by the Templars. 12th-13th cent. *Inner Temple OPEN 10.00-11.30 & 14.30-16.00 Mon-Fri. CLOSED weekends, B. Hols & legal vacations. Middle Temple OPEN 10.00-12.00 & 15.00-16.30 Mon-Fri, 10.00-16.00 Sat. CLOSED Sun, B. Hols and during examinations.*

Temple of Mithras, Bucklesbury House

Queen Victoria St EC4. Originally found 18 ft underground in Walbrook and moved here with other Roman relics.

The Tower of London

Tower Hill EC3. 01-709 0765. A keep, a prison and still a fortress. Famous for the Bloody Tower, Traitors' Gate, the ravens, Crown Jewels and the Yeomen warders. Norman Chapel of St John. *Museum OPEN Mar-Oct 09.30-17.00 Mon-Sat, 14.00-17.00 Sun; Nov-Feb 09.30-16.00 Mon-Sat. Admission charge. Jewel House OPEN Mar-Oct 09.30-17.45 Mon-Sat, 14.00-17.30 Sun; Nov-Feb 09.30-16.30 Mon-Sat. Admission charge.*

World War 2 Operational Headquarters

Whitehall SW1. 01-930 5422. A 6-acre honeycomb of rooms and corridors in the heart of government Whitehall, originally the secret war headquarters of Churchill's cabinet. War-time furnishings. *By appointment only. Write to the Chief Clerk, Cabinet Office, Whitehall SW1.*

York Watergate

Watergate Walk, off Villiers St WC2. Built in 1626 by Nicholas Stone as the watergate to York House, it marks the position of the north bank of the Thames before the construction of the Victoria Embankment in 1862. The arms and motto are those of the Villiers family.

London bridges

The tidal Thames has 17 bridges. Noteworthy ones in central London are:

Albert Bridge
Unusual rigid chain suspension. Built by Ordish 1873.

Chelsea Bridge
Original 1858. Rebuilt as suspension brigde by G. Topham Forrest & E. P. Wheeler in 1934.

London Bridge
The site of many replacements. Wooden construction until 13th cent; the famous stone bridge that followed carried houses and shops. Granite bridge built in 1832 by Rennie was shipped off to Lake Havasu City, Arizona in 1971. Latest construction completed 1973.

Tower Bridge
Victorian-Gothic towers with hydraulic twin drawbridge. Jones and Wolfe Barry 1894.

Waterloo Bridge
Concrete. Fine design by Sir Giles Gilbert Scott 1940-5.

Westminster Bridge
Graceful cast iron. Thomas Page 1862.

Historic ships

The sea has always played a major part in England's history and several historic ships are anchored along London's waterfront.

Greenwich: The 'Cutty Sark'
King William walk SE10. 01-858 3445. Stands in dry dock. One of the great sailing tea-clippers, built 1869. 'Gipsy Moth IV', the boat in which Chichester sailed round the world in 1966 stands in dry dock next to the 'Cutty Sark'. *Both ships OPEN Apr-Sept 11.00-18.00 Mon-Sat, 14.30-18.00 Sun; Oct-Mar 11.00-17.00 Mon-Sat, 14.30-17.00 Sun. CLOSED New Year's, Xmas Eve, Xmas. Small admission charge.*

HMS 'Discovery'
Victoria Embankment WC2. 01-836 5138. Captain Scott's 1901-4 Antarctica vessel. Scott relics. *OPEN 13.00-16.30. CLOSED Xmas. Free.* Other moored ships nearby are HMS 'Chrysanthemum' and HMS 'President' (naval training vessels) and the 'Wellington' belonging to the Master Mariners. *OPEN 13.00-16.30 daily. CLOSED Xmas, New Year's. Free.*

Monuments and statues

London has over 400 outdoor statues. The great majority of them are quite undistinguished; these are the best and most interesting.

Achilles
Hyde Park W1. Westmacott, 1822. Erected to honour Wellington. London's first nude statue.

Admiralty Arch
Entrance to the Mall SW1. Massive Edwardian triple arch by Sir Aston Webb 1911. A memorial to Queen Victoria.

Albert Memorial
Kensington Gore SW7. Statue of Prince Albert on a memorial to the Great Exhibition of 1851, by Sir George Gilbert Scott 1872.

Boadicea
Westminster Bridge SW1. Thornycroft, 1902. Famous group showing the ancient British Queen with her daughters in her war chariot.

The Cenotaph
Whitehall SW1. Designed 1920 by Sir Edward Lutyens to honour the dead of World War 1.

Charles I
Trafalgar Sq SW1. Le Sueur, 1633. The oldest equestrian statue in London and one of the finest. Ordered to be destroyed during the Civil War and hidden until the Restoration. It was erected on its present site between 1675 and 1677.

Cleopatra's Needle
Victoria Embankment SW1. From Heliopolis. 1500 BC. Presented by Egypt and set up by the Thames 1878.

Eros
Piccadilly Circus W1. Gilbert, 1833. Officially the Angel of Christian Charity. It is part of the memorial to the Victorian philanthropist Lord Shaftesbury. Made in aluminium.

George IV
Trafalgar Sq WC2. Chantrey, 1843. Rides without boots on a horse without saddle or stirrups. Was originally intended for the top of Marble Arch.

The Monument
Monument St EC3. A 17th cent hollow fluted column by Wren to commemorate the Great Fire of London. Magnificent view. *OPEN Mar-Sept 09.00-17.40 Mon-Sat, 14.00-17.40 Sun; Oct-Mar 09.00-16.00 Mon-Sat. CLOSED Sun, Xmas, Box, G. Fri. Admission charge.*

Nelson's Column
Trafalgar Square SW1. 145-ft-high column by William Railton 1840. Weighs 16 tons. At the top a statue of Nelson by Bailey 1843.

Peter Pan
Kensington Gardens W2. Frampton, 1912. Charming fairy figure. Erected overnight as a surprise for the children.

Queen Elizabeth I
St Dunstan in the West, Fleet St EC4. Originally stood over Lud Gate. Made during the Queen's lifetime in 1586, it is one of London's oldest statues.

Royal Artillery Memorial
Hyde Park Corner SW1. Jagger. London's best war memorial, with its great stone howitzer aimed at the Somme where the men it commemorates lost their lives. The bronze figures of soldiers are possibly the finest sculptures to be seen in the streets of London.

Victoria Memorial
In front of Buckingham Palace SW1. Brock, 1911. Impressive memorial to Queen Victoria which includes a fine dignified figure of the Queen, the best of the many statues of her.

Duke of Wellington
Hyde Park Corner SW1. Boehm, 1888. Equestrian statue of the Duke. The memorial is distinguished by four well-modelled figures of soldiers in full kit. The Duke rides his favourite horse 'Copenhagen' and he looks towards Apsley House, in which he lived.

Whittington Stone
Highgate Hill N6, near junction with Dartmouth Park Hill. Milestone marking the spot where tradition says young Dick Whittington rested on his way home from London and heard Bow Bells ring out. 'Turn again Whittington, thrice Lord Mayor of London', and returned to become London's most famous Mayor.

Houses of famous people

As you walk round London, look out for the round blue plaques which you will see here and there on the sides of houses in historic parts of town.

Carlyle's house
24 Cheyne Row SW3. 01-352 7087. A modest 18th cent street house where Carlyle lived for 42 years until his death in 1881. *OPEN 11.00-13.00 & 14.00-18.00 Wed-Sat, 14.00-18.00 Sun. CLOSED Dec & G. Fri. Admission charge.*

Dickens house
48 Doughty St WC1. 01-405 2127. 19th cent terrace house. Relics of Dickens' life and writings. He lived here from 1837 to 1839. *OPEN 10.00-17.00. CLOSED Sun, B. Hols. Admission charge.*

Hogarth's house
Hogarth Lane, Gr West Rd W4. 01-570 7728. The 17th cent country villa of William Hogarth; relics and late impressions of his engravings. *OPEN 11.00-18.00 Mon-Sat, 14.00-18.00 Sun. CLOSED at 16.00 Oct-Mar, G. Fri, Xmas Eve, Box. Small admission charge.*

Dr Johnson's house
17 Gough Square, Fleet St EC4. 17th cent house. Relics and contemporary portraits. He lived here from 1748 to 1759. *OPEN 10.30-17.00 Mon-Sat May-Sept; 10.30-16.30 Oct-Apr. CLOSED Sun, B. Hols. Small admission charge.*

Keats' house
Wentworth Place, Keats Grove NW3. 01-435 2062. The poet lived here during his prolific period 1818-20. *OPEN 10.00-18.00 Mon-Sat, 14.00-17.00 Sun. CLOSED G. Fri, Easter Sat, Xmas, Box, New Year's. Free.*

Wellington Museum
Apsley House, 149 Piccadilly W1. 01-499 5676. Known as 'No. 1 London'. Duke of Wellington's house. Built 1771-8 from designs by Robert Adam and altered 1828 by B. D. Wyatt. Contains Wellington relics, fine Spanish (Velasquez) and Dutch paintings, silver plate and porcelain. *OPEN 10.00-18.00 Mon-Sat, 14.30-18.00 Sun. CLOSED G. Fri, Xmas. Small admission charge.*

Wesley's house & chapel
47 City Rd EC1. 01-253 2262. John Wesley's possessions and personal relics. His tomb is in the chapel grounds. *OPEN 10.00-13.00 & 14.00-16.00. CLOSED Sun. G. Fri, B. Hols, Xmas, Box. Small admission charge.*

Churches

London's churches fared badly in both the 'Great Fire' of 1666 and the blitz of World War 2. Yet those remaining, restored or rebuilt, are not only surprisingly numerous but form a remarkably fine collection well worth visiting. Here are some of the most interesting.

Abbeys and cathedrals

St Paul's Cathedral
EC4. 01-248 4619. Wren's greatest work; built 1675-1710 replacing the previous church destroyed by the Great Fire. Superb dome, porches and funerary monuments. Contains magnificent stalls by Grinling Gibbons. Ironwork by Tijou, paintings by Thornhill and mosaics by Salviati and Stephens. *OPEN Apr-Sept 07.45-19.00; Oct-Mar 07.45-17.00. Crypt & galleries OPEN 10.45-15.15 Mon-Sat.*

Southwark Cathedral
Borough High St SE1. 01-407 2939. Much restored. Built by Augustinian Canons 1206. Beautiful early English choir and retrochoir. Tower built *c*. 1520, nave by Blomfield 1894-97. Contains work by Comper (altar screen).

Westminster Abbey
(The Collegiate Church of St Peter in Westminster) Broad sanctuary SW1. 01-222 1051. Original church by Edward the Confessor 1065. Rebuilding commenced by Henry III in 1245 who was largely influenced by the new French cathedrals. Completed by Henry Yevele and others 1376-1506 (towers incomplete and finished by Hawksmoor 1734). Henry VII Chapel added 1503; fine perpendicular with wonderful fan vaulting. The Abbey contains the Coronation Chair, and many tombs and memorials of the Kings and Queens of England and their subjects. Starting place for pilgrimage to Canterbury Cathedral. *Abbey OPEN 09.00-17.00 Mon-Fri. Royal Chapels OPEN various times as are the Chapter House & Chamber of the Pyx & Museum.*

Westminster Roman Catholic Cathedral
Ashley Place SW1. 01-834 7452. Early Christian Byzantine-style church by J. F. Bentley, 1903. The most important Roman Catholic church in England. Fine marbled interior.

Brompton Oratory
Brompton Rd SW7. 01-589 4811. Large Italian

Renaissance-style church designed by H. Gribble, 1884. Fine marbled interior and original statues from the Cathedral of Siena.

Chapel Royal of St John

White Tower, Tower of London EC3. The oldest church in London, *c*. 1085, original Norman.

Holy Trinity

Sloane St SW1. 01-730 2442. By Sedding in 1890. London's most elaborate church of the 'Arts and Crafts' movement.

The Queen's Chapel, St James's Palace

Marlborough Rd SW1. Built by Inigo Jones 1623. Fine restored woodwork and coffered ceiling. *OPEN on application to the Administrative Officer, Marlborough House, SW1.*

St Bartholomew-the-Great

West Smithfield EC1. 01-606 5171. Norman choir of Augustinian Priory 1123 with later Lady Chapel; the only pre-Reformation font in City. Tomb of founder (who also founded St Bartholomew's Hospital and other fine monuments.

St Clement Danes

Strand WC2. 01-242 8282. First built for the Danes, 9th cent. Spire by Gibbs. Rebuilt by Wren 1681. Destroyed in air raids 1941 and rebuilt and rededicated in 1958 as the central church of the R.A.F. Bells ring 'Oranges and Lemons' every 3 hrs. Fine moulded plaster roof.

St Martin-in-the-Fields

Trafalgar Sq WC2. 01-930 1862. James Gibbs. 1726. Famous spire and portico. Fine venetian east window and white and gold moulded plaster ceiling. Lunchtime music *13.00-14.00 Mon & Tues.*

St Paul Covent Garden

Covent Garden WC2. 01-836 5221. Fine 'ecclesiastical barn' by Inigo Jones. Rebuilt by T. Hardwick after fire of 1795. Pleasant gardens at western (entrance) end.

St Peter-upon-Cornhill

Bishopsgate Corner EC3. 01-626 9483. Very fine church by Wren, 1677-87. Oldest church site in City, reputedly AD 179. Famous for Elizabethan music: organ built by Schmidt. Fine carved screen. 14th and 15th cent plays performed at Christmas.

St Stephen Walbrook

Walbrook EC4. 01-626 2277. Masterpiece by Wren, 1672-79; steeple 1714-17. Dome, with eight arches, supported by Corinthian pillars, all beautifully restored. Fine fittings. Glass by Keith New. Lord Mayor of London's church and the home since 1953 of 'The Samaritans' to help the suicidal and desperate.

The great museums and galleries

London's national museums and galleries contain some of the richest treasures in the world. Apart from the museums owned by the nation, London is further enriched by other collections open to the public. Most were started as specialist collections of wealthy men or associations but are now available to all, by right of courtesy. They are continually being improved and extended and are an invaluable part of our culture and history.

British Museum
Gt Russell St WC1. 01-636 1555. One of the largest and greatest museums in the world. Contains famous collections of Egyptian, Assyrian, Greek and Roman, British, Oriental and Asian antiquities. Among many outstanding and unique items are the Egyptian mummies, the colossal Assyrian bulls and lions in the Nimrud gallery. Cambodian and Chinese collections, the Elgin Marbles and the Rosetta Stone. Building 1823-47 by Sir Robert Smirke; the domed reading room 1857 is by Sidney Smirke. *OPEN 10.00-17.00 Mon-Sat, 14.30-18.00 Sun. CLOSED G. Fri, Xmas, Box, New Year's. Lecture tours. Free.*

British Museum: Dept. of Ethnography
6 Burlington Gardens W1. 01-437 2224. Exciting collection of primitives, including the Benin bronzes. *Opening times as the British Museum.*

Dulwich College Picture Gallery
College Rd SE21. 01-693 5254. English, Italian, Dutch and French paintings exhibited in one of the most beautiful art galleries in England. Notable works by Rembrandt, Rubens and Gainsborough. Building by Sir John Soane 1811-14. *OPENING times vary throughout the year. CLOSED Mon, B. Hols. Free.*

Geological Museum
Exhibition Rd SW7. 01-589 3444. Physical and economic geology and mineralogy of the world; regional geology of Britain. Models, dioramas and a large collection of gems, stones and fossils. *OPEN 10.00-18.00 Mon-Sat, 14.00-17.00 Sun. CLOSED G. Fri, Xmas, Box. Free.*

The Iveagh Bequest, Kenwood
Hampstead Lane NW3. 348 1286. Fine house by Robert Adam. Paintings by Rembrandt, Vermeer, Reynolds and Gainsborough. *OPEN Apr-Sept 10.00-19.00; Oct-Mar times vary. CLOSED G. Fri, Xmas Eve, Xmas. Free.*

Museum of London
London Wall EC2. 01-600 3699. Combined collections of the former London Museum and Guildhall Museum with extra material. A 3-dimensional biography of the City and London area, with models, reconstructions and even the Lord Mayor's Coach. *OPEN Tue-Sat 10.00-18.00, Sun 14.00-18.00.*

National Gallery
Trafalgar Sq WC2. 01-839 3321. Very fine representative collection of the various schools of painting. Includes many world famous pictures. Rich in early Italian (Leonardo da Vinci, Raphael, Botticelli, and Titian). Dutch and Flemish (Rembrandt, Rubens, Frans Hals, Van Dyck), Spanish 15-18th cent (Velasquez and El Greco), British 18th and 19th cent (Constable, Turner, Gainsborough and Reynolds). Building 1838 by W. Wilkins. *Open 10.00-18.00 Mon-Sat, 14.30-18.00 Sun. CLOSED public hols. Free.*

National Portrait Gallery
2 St Martin's Place WC2. 01-930 8511. Historical collection of contemporary portraits of famous British men and women from early 9th cent to the present day. Excellent reference section of engravings and photographs. *OPEN 10.00-17.00 Mon-Fri, 10.00-18.00 Sat, 14.00-18.00 Sun. CLOSED B. Hols. Free.*

Natural History Museum
Cromwell Rd SW7. 01-589 6323. The national collections of zoology, entomology, palaeontology and botany. Particularly notable are the bird gallery, the 90-ft model blue whale and the great dinosaur models. Built 1881 by A. Waterhouse. *OPEN 10.00-18.00 Mon-Sat, 14.30-18.00 Sun. CLOSED G. Fri, Xmas. Free.*

Science Museum
Exhibition Rd SW7. 01-589 6371. The history of science and its application to industry. A large collection of very fine engineering models, steam engines, motor cars, areoplanes and all aspects of applied physics and chemistry. Instructive children's gallery. *OPEN 10.00-18.00 Mon-Sat, 14.30-18.00 Sun. CLOSED B. Hols. Free lectures 13.00 Mon, Wed & Fri, 15.00 Sat. Free.*

Tate Gallery
Millbank SW1. 01-828 1212. Representative collections
of British painting from the 16th cent to the present
day; fine examples of Blake, Turner, Hogarth, the pre-
Raphaelites, Ben Nicholson, Spenser and Francis
Bacon. Also a particularly rich collection of foreign
paintings and sculpture from 1880 to the present day,
including paintings by Picasso, Chagall, Mondrian,
Pollock, Lichtenstein, Moore, Hepworth, Degas,
Marini and Giacometti. Built 1897 by Sidney H. J.
Smith. *OPEN 10.00-18.00 Mon-Sat, 14.00-18.00 Sun.
CLOSED G. Fri, Xmas, Box. Lectures at various times.
Free.*

Victoria & Albert Museum
Cromwell Rd SW7. 01-589 6371. A museum of
decorative art, comprising vast collections from all
categories, countries and ages. Over 10 acres of
museum! Each category is extensive and choice. It
includes important collections of paintings, sculpture,
graphics and typography, armour and weapons,
carpets, ceramics, clocks, costumes, fabrics, furniture,
jewellery, metalwork and musical instruments. Fine Art
collections include Sandby, Girtin, Cotman, Constable
Turner and some Raphael cartoons. The Prints and
Drawings Dept has extensive collections dealing with
art, architecture, pure and applied design, graphics,
typography and craft. *OPEN 10.00-18.00 Mon-Sat,
14.30-17.50 Sun. CLOSED B. Hols, public hols. Free
lectures at various times. Free.*
Wallace Collection
Hertford House, Manchester Sq W1. 01-935 0687. A
private collection of outstanding works of art which
were bequeathed to the nation by Lady Wallace in
1897. Splendid representation of the French 17th and
18th cent, including many paintings by Boucher,
Watteau and Fragonard. There are also several
Rembrandts, a Titian, some Rubens, and paintings by
Canaletto and Guardi. Important collections of French
furniture. Sèvres porcelain, Majolica, Limoges enamel
and armour. Also a fine collection of Bonnington oils
and watercolours. *OPEN 10.00-17.00 Mon-Sat, 14.00-
17.00 Sun. CLOSED G. Fri, Xmas. Free.*

The royal parks

London is particularly rich in parks, gardens, commons, forests and heathland. There are over 80 parks within 7 miles of Piccadilly. The 10 Royal parks are still the property of the Crown and were originally the grounds of Royal homes or palaces.

Greenwich Park SE10
01-858 2608. A Royal park of 200 acres with pleasant avenues lined with chestnut trees, sloping down to the Thames. Impressive views of the river, the shipping and the two classical buildings; the Queen's House by Inigo Jones and the Royal Naval College (once a Tudor Royal Palace). Contains also the old Royal Observatory and its pleasant garden. 13 acres of wooded deer park, a bird sanctuary and Bronze-age tumuli. *OPEN 07.00-22.00 summer; 07.00-18.00 or dusk winter.*

Hampton Court & Bushy Park, Middx
01-977 1328. 1,100 acres of Royal park bounded on two sides by the Thames. Hampton is the formal park of a great Tudor palace with ancient courts, superb flower gardens, the famous maze and the 'great vine' planted during Queen Anne's reign. Bushy Park is natural farmland, artificial plantation, watercress and ponds. Both parks have many fine avenues including the mile-long Chestnut Avenue with 'Diana' fountain in Bushy Park. Hampton Court, itself is described under 'Historic Buildings'. *OPEN 7.45-dusk.*

Hyde Park W1
01-262 5484. A Royal park since 1536, it was once part of the forest reserved by Henry VIII for hunting wild boar and bulls. Queen Elizabeth I held military reviews here (still held on special occasions). It was the haunt of highwaymen until 1750 and even today is patrolled at night by police. The Great Exhibition of 1851 designed by Paxton was held opposite Prince of Wales Gate. Hyde Park now has 340 acres of parkland, walks, Rotten row with horse-riders, and the Serpentine — a fine natural lake for fishing, boating and swimming. The Serpentine Bridge is by George Rennie 1826. The famous 'Speaker's Corner' is near Marble Arch — public executions were held at Tyburn gallows nearby until 1783. Good open-air bar and restaurant overlooking the lake (near the bridge). *OPEN 05.00-24.00. No cars after dusk. The Lido OPEN May-Sept & hols 06.00-09.00 for swimming. Small admission charge.*

Kensington Gardens W2

01-262 5484. A formal and elegant addition to Hyde Park. 275 acres of Royal park containing William III's lovely Kensington Palace, Queen Anne's Orangery, the peaceful 'Sunken Garden' nearby, the Round Pond with its busy model sailing-boats, and, on the south, the magnificently Victorian 'Albert Memorial'. The famous Broad Walk, until recently flanked by ancient elms is now replanted with fragrant limes and maples and the nearby 'Flower Walk' is the home of wild birds, woodpeckers, flycatchers and tree-creepers. Queen Caroline produced both the Long Water (Peter Pan's statue is here) and the Serpentine by damming the Westbourne river. Good children's playground. *OPEN 05.00-dusk.*

Regents Park NW1

01-935 1537. A Royal park of 470 acres, it was originally part of Henry VIII's great hunting forest in the 16th cent. The Prince Regent in 1811 planned to connect the park (and a new palace) via the newly built Regent Street to Carlton House. Although never fully completed the design by John Nash (1812-26) is of great distinction, the park being surrounded by handsome Regency terraces and imposing gateways. Contains also the Zoo, the Regent's canal, a fine boating lake with 30 species of birds and the very fine Queen Mary's rose garden within Nash's Inner Circle. Open-air theatre. *OPEN 05.00-dusk.*

Richmond Park, Surrey

01-940 0654. A Royal park of 2,500 acres first enclosed as a hunting ground by Charles I in 1637. Retains all the qualities of a great English feudal estate — a natural open park of spinneys and plantations, bracken and ancient oaks (survivors of the great oak forests of the Middle Ages) and over 600 red and fallow deer. Badgers, weasels and the occasional fox can be seen. *OPEN Mar-Sept 07.00-dusk; 07.30-dusk winter.*

St James's Park & Green Park SW1

01-262 5484. The oldest Royal park, acquired in 1532 by Henry VIII, laid out in imitation 'Versailles' style by Charles II; finally redesigned in the grand manner for George IV by John Nash in the 1820's. A most attractive park, with fine promenades and walks, and a romantic Chinese-style lake, bridge, and weeping willows. The bird sanctuary on Duck Island has some magnificent pelicans and over 20 species of duck and geese. Good views of Buckingham Palace, the grand sweep of Carlton Terrace, the domes and spires of Whitehall and to the south, Westminster Abbey. The Mall and Constitution Hill are frequently part of ceremonial Royal occasions. *OPEN 05.00-24.00*

Zoos and aquaria

The London Zoo
Regent's Park NW1. 01-722 3333. This famous zoo has one of the largest collections of animals in the world. Excellent aviary designed by Lord Snowdon and a new 'Moonlight Hall' where day and night is reversed and rarely seen nocturnal animals are awake. The zoo was originally laid out by Decimus Burton in 1827; since then many famous architects have designed special animal houses. A large ape and monkey house opened in May '72, houses Guy the gorilla, and his mate Louie. *OPEN 09.00-dusk; Nov-Feb 10.00-16.00, 09.00-19.00 Sun & B. Hols. CLOSED Xmas. Admission charge.*

The London Zoo Aquarium
Regent's Park NW1. 01-722 3333. Marine and Tropical Halls. Excellently lit and displayed. A well-stocked aquarium of both sea and freshwater fish and amphibians from European and tropical waters. Particularly notable are the fine sea fish, the octopus, stingrays and sharks. *OPEN 09.00-dusk; Nov-Feb 10.00-16.00, 09.00-19.00 Sun & B. Hols. CLOSED Xmas. Admission charge.*

Longleat Lion Reserve
Warminster, Wilts. Maiden Bradley 328. Visitors to the magnificent Renaissance house can choose to drive through the game park where lions roam at will! You can stop your car and watch in safety but it is extremely foolhardy to get out, however friendly the lions. Also has a chimpanzee island. No soft-topped cars allowed. *OPEN 10.00-dusk. Admission charge.*

Whipsnade Park Zoo
Dunstable, Bedfordshire. Whipsnade 872171. A 500-acre 'natural' Zoo of woods and downland in the Chilterns. 2,000 animals in large open-air enclosures. Some species roam freely throughout the park. You can picnic in the grounds — take binoculars or use the telescopes provided. Travel within the park in your own car or by miniature motor-coach train. London 35 miles (M1). *OPEN 10.00-19.00 or dusk. CLOSED Xmas. Admission charge.*

Windsor Safari Park
St Leonards, Windsor. Windsor 69841. Drive round the park in the car (long queues in summer). Lion and baboon reserves, monkey jungle, zebra, camels, giraffes, and lakes with waterfowl and a reptile house. Dolphins give hourly performances in the Dolphinarium. *OPEN 10.00-dusk. CLOSED Xmas. Admission charge.*

Lo☺☺king at London

London from the water

Trips on the Thames

During the summer months daily services run from the following piers:

Charing Cross
Victoria Embankment WC2. 01-839 5320. Trips to the Tower *approx. every ½ hr;* to Greenwhich *every 45 mins.*

Tower Pier
Tower Hill EC3. 01-709 9697. Trips to Greenwich approx. *every 25 mins;* to Westminster *every 25 mins.*

Westminster Pier
Victoria Embankment SW1. 01-930 2074. Trips to Kew *every ½ hr,* to Putney & Richmond and Hampton Court *every ½ hr.*

Trips on the canal

Jason's Trip & Argonaut Gallery
Opposite 60 Blomfield Rd W9. 01-286 3428. The traditional narrow boats 'Jason' and 'Serpens' leave the Argonaut Gallery for 1½ hr return trips, with commentary, through Regent's Park and zoo to Hampstead Road locks. *Depart 11.00, 14.00, 18.00.* Night trips *depart 19.30.* Booked parties only £2.75 including supper and music.

Jenny Wren Cruises
Camden Lock, Commercial Place, Chalk Farm Rd NW1. 01-485 6210. 1½ hr round trips along Regent's Canal passing the Zoo and Little Venice. Up to 4 tours a day *daily from Easter to end Sep.* Also longer and evening trips.

Zoo Water Bus
British Waterways Board, Delamere Terrace W2. 01-286 6101. Boat leaves from the end of Delamere Terrace for ½ hr trip to the zoo. *On the hour 10.00-17.00 (Sun and B. Hols till 18.00). Last return boat leaves zoo 17.45 (Sun and B. Hols till 18.45).* Visit to the zoo optional.

Viewpoints

A nice way of orientating oneself or seeing London with a fresh sense of alignment is to go to the top of one of the very tall, new buildings. Together with old favourites and natural viewpoints, these are the most outstanding

Hampstead Heath
450 ft high. Constable's famous view of London. A more comfortable view from:
Jack Straw's Castle
North End Way NW3. 01-435 8885. Lunch and dinner in the restaurant with long views across London to the distant Kentish hills. *CLOSES 20.00 LD (Sun L only)*
London Hilton
Park Lane W1. 01-493 8000. Roof bar at 320 ft. Lift. Fine views on Hyde Park, Buckingham Palace and Mayfair.
Post Office Tower
Cleveland St W1. 01-636 9361. The highest restaurant in London, revolving slowly and giving an ever-changing view over Regent's Park, central and outer London: from Epping Forest in the east to the Surrey hills in the west.
St Paul's Cathedral
EC4. Magnificent view of the City, the Wren churches, the Tower and London Pool. 335 ft. 727 steps. *OPEN Mon-Sat 10.45-15.15 (& 16.45-18.80 Summer only).* Small admission charge to see the galleries.

Daily ceremonies

These are the main ceremonies that occur daily throughout the year. For information about individual day's events dial Teletourist service (see under Information centres).

The Changing of the Queen's Guard
Buckingham Palace SW1
The new Guard, following the band, arrives from Chelsea or Wellington Barracks for ceremony lasting ½hr. Not held in bad weather. *Daily 11.30, alternate days in winter.*
The old Guard leaves St James's for Buckingham Palace at *11.15.* Small ceremony.

The Changing of the Queen's Life Guard
Horse Guards Arch, Whitehall SW1.
The ceremony popularly known as 'the changing of the Guard' lasts 20 mins. *11.00 (Sun 10.00)*. The Guard is also inspected on foot at *16.00*.
The Changing of the Guard
Windsor Castle, Windsor Berks.
A new Guard relieves the old Guard *every day at 10.30*.
A military band enlivens the pageant.
Ceremony of the Keys
Tower of London EC3
The Chief Warder, with an escort of soldiers bearing arms, locks the West Gates and the Middle Tower and Byward Tower doors with traditional ceremony. *21.40 by written application to the Governor.*

Seasonal events in London

The following list presents not only the most important annual events but also some of the more obscure London customs in order to cover as wide a field as possible.
Some, like the Trooping of the Colour, or the State Opening of Parliament, are attended by the Queen. The Royal Family's daily schedule is published in the Court Circular in 'The Times' or 'Daily Telegraph'. Other dignitaries like the Lord Mayor or the Prime Minister also appear at ceremonials as well as in their official roles at the Mansion House or the Houses of Parliament.
For exact dates, times and places, where not given, contact one of the centres given under 'information centres'.

Spring

Chinese New Year
Soho, Gerrard St W1. Papier-mâché dragon and lit-up festivities march through the centre of London's Chinese community. *Jan or Feb.*
Cruft's Dog Show
Olympia. *Early Feb.*
Royal Film Performance
A selected film gets royal patronage in aid of charity. Celebrities and glitter at one of the big cinemas. *No fixed date.*

Spring Antiques Fair
Chelsea Old Town Hall, Kings Rd SW3. 01-352 8101. *Mid Mar.*

Oxford v Cambridge Boat Race
River Thames, Putney to Mortlake. *Mar or April.*

Easter Sunday Parade
Battersea Park SW11. Colourful carnival procession preceded by a parade of old vehicles. *Easter Sun.*

Easter Procession & Carols
Westminster Abbey SW1. 01-222 1051. *Easter Mon.*

London Harness Horse Parade
Regent's Park NW1. Fine horses and carts; brewer's vans and drays on parade. Judging *starts at 09.45* followed by a procession twice round the Inner Circle *at about 12.00. Easter Mon.*

Putney & Hammersmith Amateur Regattas
01-748 3632. Rowing regattas make exciting watching from the river banks.

May Day
Labour Party procession to Hyde Park W1. *1st May.*

Summer Art Exhibition
Royal Academy, Burlington House, Piccadilly W1. 01-734 9052. *May-end of July.*

F.A. Cup Final
Empire Stadium, Wembley, Middx. 01-902 1234. The climax of the English football season. *2nd Sat in May.*

Chelsea Flower Show
Royal Hospital Grounds, Chelsea SW3. 01-730 7036. Superb flower displays. *For 3 days late May. No fixed date.*

Rugby League Challenge Cup Final
Wembley. *Mid May.*

Summer

Royal Ascot Races
A fashionable society event where hats attract more attention than the horses.

The Garter Ceremony
Service, attended by the Queen at St George's Chapel, Windsor, preceded by a colourful procession with the Household Cavalry and Yeomen of the Guard. Ceremony dates from 14th cent. *Mon afternoon of Ascot week (usually third week in June).*

Antique Dealers Fair & Exhibition
Grosvenor House, Park Lane W1. 01-499 6363. *Mid June.*

Trooping the Colour
The route is from Buckingham Palace SW1 along the Mall to Horse Guards Parade, Whitehall and back again. Pageantry at its best for the Queen's official birthday. *11.00, Sat nearest 11th June.*

Lord's Test Match
Lord's Cricket Ground, St John's Wood Rd NW8. Tickets 01-289 1615. Prospects of play 01-286 8011. *June or July.*

Election of Sheriffs of the City of London
Guildhall EC2. 01-606 3030. Lord Mayor and Aldermen in a colourful ceremony. Posies are carried traditionally to ward off 'the plague'. *24th June.*

All England Lawn Tennis Championships
All England Lawn Tennis & Croquet Club, Church Rd, Wimbledon SW19. 01-946 2244. 'Wimbledon Fortnight', the world's most famous championship. *Last week in June and first week July.*

Royal Tournament March Past
Horseguards, Whitehall SW1. Colourful parade by all troops taking part in the Royal Tournament. *15.00 Sun before Tournament.*

Royal Tournament
Earls Court. 01-385 1200. Impressive military spectacle with marching displays and massed brass bands. *Mid July 2 weeks. No fixed date.*

Royal International Horse Show
Empire Pool, Wembley, Middx. 01-902 1234. Top-class show jumping competition before Royalty. *Mid July. No fixed date.*

Doggetts Coat & Badge Race
The Thames, London Bridge to Chelsea. Rowing race for Thames Watermen, originated in 1715. Sometimes called the 'Waterman's Derby'. *Mid July or early Aug. No fixed date.*

Henry Wood Promenade Concerts
Royal Albert Hall, Kensington Gore SW7. 01-589 8212. Concerts of classical music. Tickets by ballot only for first and last nights. *Late July until Sep. No fixed date.*

Bank Holiday Fair
Hampstead Heath (nr North End way) NW3. *B. Hol Mon.*

Autumn

Battle of Britain Week
Thanksgiving service at Westminster Abbey SW1. 01-222 1051. Biggin Hill Flying Display. *Early Sept.*

Harvest of the Sea Thanksgiving
St Mary at Hill, Lovat Lane EC3. 01-626 4184. Also a fine display of fish at the church. *11.00, 2nd Sun in Oct.*

Costermongers' Harvest Festival
St Martin-in-the-Fields, Trafalgar Square WC2. 01-930 1862. Service attended by the 'Pearly Kings and Queens', in their colourful regalia. *15.30, 1st Sun in Oct.*

International Motor Fair
Earls Court. Popular and crowded. Oct.

Horse of the Year Show
Wembley Stadium, Empire Way, Wembley, Middx. 01-902 1234. Fine show jumping. *Early Oct.*

Winter

London to Brighton Veteran Car Run: Start
Hyde Park corner W1. Vintage cars leave here for Brighton. *08.00 1st Sun Nov.*

State Opening of Parliament
The Queen, in the Irish state coach, is driven from Buckingham Palace to the House of Lords. A royal salute is fired in St James's Park. *Early Nov. No fixed date.*

Guy Fawkes Day
Anniversary of the Gunpowder Plot of 1605. Private and public firework displays. *Evening, 5th Nov.*

Admission of the Lord Mayor Elect
The Lord Mayor takes office. Colourful ceremony at Guildhall including handing over of insignia by former Lord Mayor. *Fri before* Lord Mayor's show.

Lord Mayor's Procession & Show
The newly elected Lord Mayor is driven in his state coach from the Guildhall to the Law Courts to be received by the Lord Chief Justice. The biggest ceremonial event in the City. *2nd Sat Nov.*

Armistice Day
Poppies sold in the streets to raise money for ex-servicemen. Service at the Cenotaph, Whitehall SW1 with a salute of guns. *11.00. 2nd Sun Nov.*

Royal Command Performance
London Palladium, Argyle St WC1. Variety show in aid of charity occasionally attended by the Queen.

Annual Ice Show
Empire Pool, Wembley, Middx. 01-902 1234. Pantomime on ice. *Dec-Mar.*

Tower of London Church Parades
Tower of London EC3. The Yeomen warders in state dress are inspected and parade before and after morning service on the *Sun before Xmas 11.00. Also Easter Sun & Whit Sun.*

Westminster Carol Service
Carol services *on 26th, 27th and 28th Dec.*

New Year's Eve
Trafalgar Square WC2. Singing of 'Auld Lang Syne' by massed crowds also dancing around (sometimes in) the fountains.
St Paul's Cathedral EC4
Gathering of Scots outside. *22.00-24.00. 31st Dec.*

LONDON NIGHTLIFE

Night clubs

London's top night clubs are expensive, but the facilities they offer are superb;membership (M) is usually necessary for entry.

Bristol Suite
14 Bruton Place W1. 01-499 1938. Hostesses, music and an international cuisine. *D OPEN 20.30-03.30 Mon-Fri.* A. Ax. B. Cb. Dc. E. **£££.**

Le Cercle
5 Hamilton Place W1. 01-499 5050. Elegant and exclusive. Dancing to an orchestra. *OPEN 18.30-02.30. CLOSED Sun.* (M). **£££.**

Clermont
44 Berkeley Square W1. 01-493 5587. Excellent restaurant and wine list.

Crockford's
16 Carlton House Terrace SW1. 01-930 2721. A. Ax. B. Dc.

Curzon House Club
21-23 Curzon St W1. 01-493 3581. Ax. Dc. B.

Palm Beach
May Fair Hotel, Berkeley St W1. 01-493 6585.

Penthouse
11 Whitehouse St W1. 01-493 1977. *OPEN 18.30-03.00. CLOSED Sun.* (M) **£££.**

Playboy
45 Park Lane W1. 01-629 6666. All the facilities to soothe the tired executive. Bunnies (untouchable), bar with pin-ups, cabaret (in the Playroom), discotheque, *OPEN 12.00-04.00.* (M) varies. **£££.**

Stork Room
99 Regent St W1. 01-734 1393. Well-established club which maintains strong nostalgic associations with the late owner, Al Burnett (noted entertainer of the '50's). Twice nightly shows with singers, dancers and two bands at *23.30 and 01.45. OPEN 21.00-04.00.* Dinner, supper & breakfast.

Discotheques

Discotheques generally cater for the affluent young, the new celebrities and the fashionable. They are very numerous; these are probably the best and most popular. Membership is often necessary.

Annabels
44 Berkeley Square W1. 01-629 2350. Fashionable but expensive club for sophisticated clientele. (M) *CLOSED Sun.* **£££**.

Dingwalls
Camden Lock, Camden High St NW1. 01-267 4967. Long room with a reasonable restaurant at one end and stage and dance floor at the other. Groups and records. Very popular. **££**.

Global Village
The Arches, Villiers St WC2. 01-839 3641. Choice of bars, music or dancing for the energetic. *OPEN to 00.30 Wed, 01.00 Thur, 03.00 Fri & Sat.* **£**.

Marquee
90 Wardour St W1. 01-437 6603. More of a music club than a disco. Younger age group. *OPEN 19.00-23.00 only.* **£**.

Playground
Hatchetts, 67a Piccadilly W1. 01-629 2001. Distinguished by its incredible décor which won first prize in an international design competition; there are carpets on the walls, zebra fur upholstery and mirrors reflecting every action. Good discotheque with frequent live groups. Snacks or full meals available. *OPEN 20.00-03.30 Mon-Fri, 20.00-24.00 Sun.* **££**.

Saddle Room
1a Hamilton Mews W1. 01-499 4994. Popular disco and restaurant. *OPEN 21.00-04.00.* (M). **£££**.

Samantha's
3 New Burlington St W1. 01-734 5425. A well known and lively place with groups and discs. *OPEN 21.00-03.00 (till 04.00 Sat); (20.00-01.30 Sun).* **££**.

Sloop John D
River Thames, Cadogan Pier SW3. 01-223 3341. Intercepters whizz you across to the floating discotheque. Good restaurant. *OPEN 20.00-03.00 Tues-Sat.* Disco *22.00-03.00.* (M). **££**

Thursdays
38 Kensington High St W8. 01-937 7744. Popular non-membership club. Large complex includes 4 bars, a good dance floor and restaurant. Jeans banned. *OPEN Mon-Sat 21.00-03.00.* **££**.

Tiffany's
22 Shaftesbury Avenue W1. 01-437 5012. Resident group and records. *OPEN 20.00-02.00 Mon-Thur, 20.00-03.00 Fri & Sat, 19.30-24.00 Sun.* **££**

Dinner dancing

Differs from the previous section with the emphasis on the food as opposed to the music, which is either in a separate room or at a lower volume than in the discotheques. No membership is necessary.

Beachcomber
May Fair Hotel, Berkeley Square W1. 01-629 7777. Polynesian theme, tropical drinks, alligators in a pool. *OPEN 19.30-02.00. CLOSED Sun.* A. Ax. B. Dc. E. **£££.**

Celebrity
13 Clifford St, New Bond St W1. 01-493 7636. Resident groups. Cabaret stars at *22.30 and 01.30. OPEN 20.00-03.00. CLOSED Sun.* A. Ax. B. Cb. Dc. E. **££.**

Churchill's
160 New Bond St W1. 01-493 2626. Long established traditional night club. Cabaret (usually several acts) and floorshow at *23.00 and 01.00. OPEN 21.00-04.00. CLOSED Sun.* A. Ax. B. Cb. Dc. E. **£££.**

Eve
189 Regent St W1. 01-734 0557. Luxurious surroundings and glittering floor shows. Excellent French cooking. Floor show *22.45, 00.45 & 01.45. D OPEN to 03.30. CLOSED Sun.* A. Ax. B. Dc. E. **£££.**

Latin Quarter
13 Wardour St W1. 01-437 6001. Resident floor show and band. *OPEN 20.00-03.30. CLOSED Sun.* A. Ax B. Cb. Dc. E. **£££.**

Quaglino's
16 Bury St SW1. 01-930 6767. Tasteful, professional and very much part of the 'establishment'. Two bands. Imaginative food. *OPEN 19.30-01.30. CLOSED Sun.* A. Ax. B. Cb. Dc. E. **£££.**

Roof Restaurant
Hilton Hotel, Park Lane W1. 01-493 8000. The view is all you would imagine, the décor light and modern. Two bands. French food. *OPEN 19.30-01.00.* A. Ax. B. Dc. E. **£££.**

Showboat
Trafalgar Square Corner House WC2. 01-930 2781. Theatre restaurant with revue, dancing. Popular prices. *OPEN 20.30-01.00. CLOSED Sun.* **££.**

Savoy Restaurant
Savoy Hotel, Strand WC2. 01-836 4343. Elegant, formal. Resident orchestra and cabaret (usually a big name singer). *OPEN 20.00-02.00. CLOSED Sun.* A. Ax. B. E. **£££**.

Talk of the Town
Hippodrome Corner, Charing Cross Rd WC2. 01-734 5051. Theatre restaurant with a resident revue and bands. International cabaret star at *23.00. OPEN 19.30 - 01.15. CLOSED Sun.* A. Ax. B. Cb. Dc. E. **£££**.

Terrace Restaurant
Dorchester Hotel, Park Lane W1. 01-629 8888. Pleasant atmosphere. Live music but no cabaret. *OPEN 20.00- 01.00. CLOSED Sun.* Dinner à la carte. A. Ax. B. Dc. E. **£££**.

Tiddy Dol's
2 Hertford St W1. 01-499 2357. An 18th cent house in Shepherd Market. Excellent game and English dishes with dancing in the Minstrel's Gallery. *D OPEN to 03.00.* A. Ax. B. Cb. Dc. E. **££**.

Villa Dei Cesari
135 Grosvenor Rd SW1. 01-828 7453. Converted riverside warehouse with a fine view over the Thames. Continental food. Dance floor with one band. *OPEN 19.30-02.30. CLOSED Mon.* Dinner à la carte. Ax. B. Dc. E. **£££**.

Jazz clubs

100 Club
100 Oxford St W1. 01-636 0933. Lively, noisy, British jazz and room to dance. *OPEN 19.30-24.00 Sun-Thur, 19.30-01.00 Fri & Sat.*

Madingly Club
Richmond Bridge, Surrey. 01-892 5818. Trad jazz on *Thur & Sun* in this lovely riverside club.

Ronnie Scott's
47 Frith St W1. 01-439 0747. The best jazz in London backed by the right blend of good food, comfort and subtle lighting. On the stand a succession of big name jazzmen, usually USA imports. *OPEN 20.30-03.00. CLOSED Sun.*

Ticket agents

Keith Prowse
24 Store St WC1. 01-836 2184. Plus many other branches. *OPEN Mon-Fri 09.30-17.30.*

Theatres, cinemas and music

London theatre is famous throughout the world for its diversity and quality. There has always been a group of favourites in the West End, but recently many avant-garde and experimental theatres have sprung up outside this traditional area. See the weekly 'Time Out' for reviews of fringe and experimental theatre and current programmes. The daily papers and 'What's On in London' have lists of current cinema and theatre.

Opera, ballet and concert halls

Coliseum
St Martin's Lane WC2. 01-836 3161. Largest London theatre seating 2,700. Now houses both the resident English National Opera (formerly Sadler's Wells Company) and the touring one.

Covent Garden Royal Opera House
Bow St WC2. 01-240 1066. Information & bookings 01-240 1911 *(24-hr service)*. World-famous ballet and opera company.

The Place
17 Duke's Rd WC1. 01-387 0031. Home of the London Contemporary Dance Theatre, an exciting and creative modern dance company. Immaculate production with interesting choreographic ideas.

Royal Albert Hall
Kensington Gore SW7. 01-589 8212. Victorian domed hall named after Prince Albert, built 1871. Orchestral, choral, pop concerts and public meetings. Famous for the 'Proms'.

Royal Festival Hall
South Bank SE1. 01-928 3191. Built in 1951 for the Festival of Britain. Seats 3,000. Orchestral and choral concerts. Forms the South Bank Arts Centre with the Queen Elizabeth Hall, Purcell Room, National Film Theatre and the Hayward Gallery.

Sadler's Wells
Rosebery Avenue EC1. 01 837 1672. Great ballet and opera by visiting companies. The original Sadler's Wells Company now play at the Coliseum, St Martin's Lane.

Wigmore Hall
36 Wigmore St W1. 01-935 2141. Instrumental, song, chamber music and orchestral recitals.

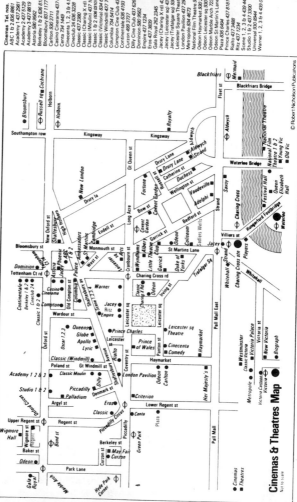

Cinemas & Theatres Map

Not to scale

● Cinemas
■ Theatres

© Robert Nicholson Publications

Theatres Tel. nos.
Adelphi 836 7611
Albery 836 3878
Aldwych 836 6404
Ambassadors 836 1171
Apollo 437 2663
Arts 836 3334
Cambridge 836 6056
Coliseum 836 3161
Comedy 930 2578
Covent Garden 240 1911/1066
Criterion 930 3216
Drury Lane 836 8108
Duchess 836 8243
Duke of York's 836 5122
Fortune 836 2238
Garrick 836 4601
Globe 437 1592
Haymarket 930 9832
Her Majesty's 930 6606
Jeanetta Cochrane Theatre 242 7040
Lit. Theatre Club 240 0660
Lyric 437 3686
May Fair 629 3036
Mermaid 248 7656
National Theatre 928 2252
New London 405 0072
New Victoria 834 2544
New Victoria 834 0671
Palace 437 6834
Palladium 437 7373
Phoenix 836 8611
Piccadilly 437 4506
Players 839 1134
Prince of Wales 930 8681
Queen Elizabeth H. 928 3191
Queen's 734 1166
Regent 323 2707
Royal Albert Hall 589 8212
Royal Festival Hall 928 3191
Royalty 405 8004
Sadler's Wells 837 1672
St. Martin's 836 1443
Savoy 836 8888
Shaftesbury 836 6596
Strand 836 2660
Talk of the Town 734 5051
Vaudeville 836 9988
Victoria Palace 834 1317
Westminster 834 0283
Whitehall 930 6692
Wigmore H. 635 2141
Wyndham's 836 3028

Cinemas Tel. nos.
ABC 1 & 2 836 8861
Academy 1 437 2981
Academy 2 437 5129
Academy 3 437 8819
Astoria 580 9562
Berkeley 1 & 2 836 8150
Bloomsbury 837 1177
Carlton 930 3711
Casino Cinerama 437 6877
Centa 734 1449
Cinecenta 1, 2, 3 & 4 930 0631
Cinecenta (McAull) 437 1653
Cineclub 28 636 3228
Classic 1 & 2 636 0310
Classic (Charing X rd) 930 6915
Classic (Victoria) 834 6588
Classic Windmill 437 7413
Columbia 734 5414
Compton Cine Club 437 4555
Continentale 636 4193
Curzon 499 3737
Dilly Cine Club 437 6266
Empire 437 1234
Eros 437 3839
Gala Royal 262 2345
Jacey (Charing X rd) 437 4815
Jacey (Leicester sq) 437 2001
Jacey (Trafalgar sq) 930 1143
Leicester Square Theatre 930 5252
London Pavilion 437 2982
Metropole 834 4673
National Film Theatre 928 3232
Odeon Haymarket 930 2738
Odeon Leicester sq 930 6111
Odeon Marble Arch 723 2011
Odeon St Martin's Lane 836 0691
Plaza 437 1234
Prince Charles 437 8181
Rialto 437 3488
Ritz 437 1234
Studio 1 & 2 3 437 3300
Universal 930 8944
Warner 1, 2, 3 & 4 439 0791

Restaurants

International

Borshtch N'Tears
45 Beauchamp Place SW3. 01-589 5003. Loud, musical and very popular Slav restaurant. Unofficial dancing and much cheer. Large menu — boeuf strogonoff, chicken kiev, lamb kebabs in vast portions. Advisable to arrive before 20.00 or after 22.00. *D Reserve for parties over 7. OPEN to 02.00.* A. Ax. B. Dc. **£.**

Brompton Grill
243 Brompton Rd SW3. 01-589 2129. Consistently good food and service. Lobster bisque, tournedos rossini, good fish and grills. Fresh fruit. *LD Reserve. OPEN to 23.00, Sun to 22.30. CLOSED Sun L.* Ax. Dc. E. **£££.**

Carrier's
2 Camden Passage N1. 01-226 5353. Owned by the gourmet Robert Carrier. Eat in either a French 19th cent inn or a gothic greenhouse in the garden. Classic dishes from the famous cook book: lamb in Greek pastry, roulade of red caviar, petit pôt au chocolat à l'orange. Table d'hôte only. *LD Reserve. OPEN to 23.30. CLOSED Sun.* **£££.**

Chanterelle
119 Old Brompton Rd SW7. 01-373 7390. Attractive décor, friendly service. Dim lights and huge helpings. Mousse of Stilton, grilled steak of lamb. Reasonable set lunch. *LD Reserve. OPEN to 24.00, Sun to 23.00. CLOSED Sun L.* Ax. **£.**

Connaught Hotel
Carlos Place W1. 01-499 7070. Smooth, discreet and unchanged. Panelled dining room or à la carte grill. Mainly English and French cuisine. Oeufs en surprise Connaught, silverside of beef, tournedos cendrillon. *LD OPEN to 22.00. CLOSED Sat D, Sun.* A. E. **£££.**

Daphne's
112 Draycott Avenue SW3. 01 589 4257. Small and dimly lit. Theatrical clientele. Very good soups. Roast grouse, veau au romarin. *D Reserve. OPEN to 24.00. CLOSED Sun.* **££.**

Inigo Jones
14 Garrick St WC2. 01-836 6456. Extremely popular restaurant in an old mission school reputedly built by the architect of the same name. First-rate food on a regularly-changed menu: smoked salmon and sour cream blinis, rognonnade d'agneau mâconnaise, soufflé chaud à la Riki. *LD Reserve. OPEN to 24.00. CLOSED Sat L, Sun.* A. Ax. B. Dc. E. **£££**.

Leith's
92 Kensington Park Rd W11. 01-229 4481. Tastefully offbeat décor in this converted private house complements the originality of the menu. Preparation, presentation and service are excellent. Leith's duckling, trout mousse, ginger syllabub. D Reserve. *OPEN to 24.00, Sun to 23.15*. A. Ax. B. Dc. E. **£££**.

Odin's
27 Devonshire St W1. 01-935 7296. Décor of umbrellas and Roman busts. Individual menu inspired by various traditions of cooking. Seasonal food: game and mussels in winter, lobster in summer. *LD Reserve. OPEN to 23.15. CLOSED Sat L & Sun.* **£££**.

Salamis
204 Fulham Rd SW10. 01-352 9827. Comfortable & relaxing offering an imaginative menu including some excellent Greek dishes. *LD Reserve. OPEN to 24.00. CLOSED Sun.* Ax. B. Dc. **£**.

American
Drones
1 Pont St SW1. 01-235 9638. Stylishly spread over two floors, offering an uncomplicated menu featuring different hamburgers, shakes and ices. *LD OPEN to 24.00.* A. Ax. B. Dc. **£**.

Maxwells
76 Heath St NW3. 01-794 5450. Eat country style fried chicken, steaks and salads with a Hawaiian touch, delicious sweets, all very good value. *LD OPEN to 00.30.* **£**.

Parsons
311 Fulham Rd SW10. 01-352 0651. Lively cafe with rock music. Generous helpings and free seconds of spaghetti, hot sandwiches, ice creams and shakes. *LD OPEN to 01.00.* **£**.

The Widow Applebaum's Deli and Bagel Academy
46 South Molton St W1. 01-629 4649. American — Jewish delicatessen with a lengthy menu offering 101 dishes. Chopped liver, matzo balls, good hot pastrami, and a large selection of sandwiches, salads, burgers, ice cream sodas and giant sundaes. *LD OPEN to 22.30. CLOSED Sun.* **£**.

Chinese Cantonese

The cooking of Canton and Southern China. Nearly all Chinese restaurants in this country are Cantonese and nearly all have unfortunately made many concessions to English taste. Cantonese when authentic is very good indeed. It differs from Pekingese mainly by being more liquid. It is steamed, boiled or braised — herbs and sauces are widely used.

The Friends

The City Friends, 34 Old Bailey EC4. 01-248 5189.
The Good Friends, 139 Salmon La E14. 01-985 5541. A family concern of excellent Cantonese restaurants. Home grown beanshoots and raw materials. Try black eggs, belly of pork with oyster, savoury duck, eels, chicken in lemon sauce, Chinese cheese. *OPEN to 24.00. Reserve.* **£.**

Lee Ho Fook

15 Gerrard St W1. 01-734 9578. Patronised by numerous Chinese for the good cooking and reasonable prices. Duck stew with abalone, sliced steak in oyster sauce, suckling pig. LD OPEN to 24.00 **£.**

Sun Luk

2 Macclesfield St W1. 01-734 5161. Cantonese cooking of a high standard — most of the customers are Chinese too. Excellent for quelling hunger pains after midnight. Wonton soup, roast duck, steamed crab, eels. *LD OPEN to 04.30.* **£.**

Chinese: Pekingese

The dishes of Peking, Formosa and Northern China are considered to be the highest form of Chinese cuisine and often equal in quality to the best French cooking. There are only about 20 genuine Pekingese restaurants in England (mostly in London). The food is drier and sharper than Cantonese (often roasted or quick fried) and the 7 to 8 courses are all eaten separately as a 'banquet' — a leisurely ceremonial occasion ideally shared between 4 to 6 people. If possible order the day before — you can leave the choice to the restaurant.

Mr Chow

151 Knightsbridge SW1. 01-589 7347. Pekingese food, with Italian overtones. Modern décor and paintings. Peking duck, sole in wine. *LD Reserve. OPEN to 23.45.* A. Ax. B. Cb. Dc. E. **£££.**

Golden Duck

6 Hollywood Rd SW10. 01-352 3500. Casual, and dimly lit. Calls itself 'London's first Chinese bistro'. Pop-art walls. Food genuinely good (banquet or à la carte). *D OPEN to 24.00. L Sat & Sun only.* Ax. B. Dc. **££.**

English

Many pubs also serve good lunches based on traditional English cooking. Refer to the section 'Pubs'.

Baker & Oven
10 Paddington St W1. 01-935 5072. A restaurant in a converted Victorian bakery. Original bakers' ovens still used to cook enormous portions of English food. Soups, pies, roasts and game, all very good. *LD Reserve. OPEN to 23.00. CLOSED Sun & Sat L.* A. Ax. B. Dc. **££**. Children.

The Bargee
Commercial Complex, Camden Lock, Chalk Farm Rd NW1. 01-485 6044. Situated in an old stable building and pleasantly decorated. Pheasant pâté with rum, prawn and mushroom salad, fresh peach mousse. *D Reserve. OPEN to 23.15, L Sat & Sun. CLOSED Mon.* A. Ax. B. Dc. **££**.

Hungry Horse
196 Fulham Rd SW10. 01-352 7757. A mirrored ceiling, wooden tables and modern décor. English cooking at its best. Home-made soups, onion and anchovy salad, calves brains, kedgeree. *LD Reserve. OPEN to 24.00. Closed last 10 days of Aug.* **££**.

Lockets
Marsham Court, Marsham St SW1. 01-834 9552. Richly panelled and dignified; popular with MPs from round the corner. Attractively presented medieval dishes. Saddle of hare, spiced beef cooked in strong ale. Fine wine list. *LD OPEN to 23.00. CLOSED Sat & Sun.* A. Ax. B. Dc. E. **£££**

Rules
35 Maiden Lane, Strand WC2. 01-836 5314. Genuine Edwardian eating house with very good traditional English food. Jellied and smoked eels, grouse pie, duckling with orange sauce. *LD OPEN to 23.15. CLOSED Sat & Sun.* **££**.

Shirreff's Restaurant & Wine Parlour
15 Great Castle St W1. 01-580 2125. English dishes at their best; oxtail, jugged hare, steak and kidney pies and puddings, braised beef. Good wine at shop prices. *LD Reserve. OPEN to 22.00. CLOSED Sat & Sun.* Ax. Dc. **£**.

Simpson's-in-the-Strand
100 Strand WC2. 01-836 9112. A famous restaurant with an Edwardian club atmosphere. The attentive service and the large carvings from enormous joints of beef and lamb are the best feature. Draught beer. *LD Reserve. OPEN to 22.00. CLOSED Sun.* **£££**.

Stone's Chop House
Panton St SW1. 01-930 0037. Victorian chop house, rebuilt after the war and given authentic atmosphere with brass, black leather seating and Victoriana. Excellent English cooking with generous helpings. Grilled meats, steak and kidney pudding and pie, roast saddle of mutton. *LD OPEN to 23.15. CLOSED Sun.* A. Ax. B. E. **££.**

Wiltons
27 Bury St SW1. 01-930 8391. Small distinguished and Edwardian with art nouveau décor. Simple and delicious English food. Oysters, lobsters, roast beef and excellent game. *OPEN to 23.00 LD. CLOSED Sun.* **£££.**

French

The following restaurants all serve classical and famous French cooking at its best.

Le Bistingo
57 Old Compton St W1. 01-437 0784. Excellent Soho bistro serving provincial French cooking from a blackboard menu. Fresh sardines, coquille de homard et scampi venison, banana au rhum. Carafes. *LD OPEN to 24.00, Sun to 23.00.* A. Ax. B. Cb. Dc. E. **£.**

Le Cellier du Midi
28 Church Row NW3. 01-435 9998. Good, well flavoured typical Midi and Languedoc food served in the cellar of a fashionable Hampstead house. Pot au feu, pousse bedaine, crème brûlée. *D Reserve. OPEN to 23.30. CLOSED Sun.* A. Ax. B. Dc. **££.**

Chez Solange
35 Cranbourn St WC2. 01-836 0542. Busy but roomy. Typical French cuisine with service entirely by women. Cerville au beurre noir, mignons de veau gratinée Lyonnaise, coq au vin. *LD Reserve. OPEN to 02.00.* A. Ax. B. Cb. Dc. **££**

Claridges
Brook St W1. 01-629 8860. Distinguished French cooking in luxurious surroundings. The atmosphere is typical of the sedate thirties. Polished service and notable wine list. *LD Reserve. OPEN to 23.00.* A.E. **£££.**

A L'Ecu de France
111 Jermyn St SW1. 01-930 2837. Superlative food. Fruits de mer, ris de Veau clarence. Notable wine list. *LD OPEN to 23.30. CLOSED Sun. L Sat.* B. Dc. **£££.**

L'Etoile
30 Charlotte St W1. 01-636 7189. Typically French in atmosphere and style. Top-quality food and attentive service. Caldeirada, rognons sautés au vin rouge, turbot à la Monégasque. Better at lunch. *LD Reserve. OPEN to 22.00. CLOSED Sat & Sun.* **£££.**

Le Gavroche
61-3 Lower Sloane St SW1. 01-730 2820. Luxury restaurant with haute cuisine. Soufflé suissesse, caneton Gavroche, omelette soufflé Rothschild. Cooking variable but service faultless. *D* Reserve. *OPEN to 24.00. CLOSED Sun.* Ax. **£££**.

Kettners
29 Romilly St W1. 01-437 3437. A 100-year old comfortably plush establishment with courteous leisurely service. Try their daily special dish. *LD OPEN to 23.15, Sun to 22.15.* A. Ax. B. Dc. **££**.

Marcel
14 Sloane St SW1. 01-235 4912. Provincial, with 'slate' specialities. Boeuf bourguignonne, coeur de filet en croûte. *LD OPEN to 22.30. CLOSED Sun.* Ac. B. Dc. **££**.

Mon Plaisir
21 Monmouth St WC2. 01-836 7243. Small, spartan, typically French bistro. Unobsequious but friendly service. Escalope à l'estragon, veau Marengo, poulet au vinaigre. *LD Reserve. OPEN to 22.00. CLOSED Sat L, Sun.* **£**.

Au Savarin
8 Charlotte St W1. 01-636 7134. One of the last original pre-war restaurants with service to match. Classical French cuisine. *LD OPEN to 22.30. Closed Sun.* **£££**.

Trencherman
271 New Kings Rd SW6. 01-736 4988. Tiled floor, French tavern decor. Family run restaurant. Bouillabaisse, suprême de volaille à la Périgord, good wine selection. *LD Reserve. OPEN to 23.15. CLOSED L Sat, D Sun.* A. Ax. B. Dc. E. **££**.

German and Austrian
Kerzerstuberl
9 St Christopher's Place W1. 01-486 3196. Authentic Austrian food and music on the accordion, with yodelling. You are expected to join in, so be prepared for a noisy evening. *LD Reserve. OPEN to 23.00. CLOSED L Sat, Sun.* A. Ax. B. Dc. **££**.

Old Vienna
94 New Bond St W1. 01-629 8716. Gay Austrian atmosphere, music and excellent cooking. Rindsbraten sacher Art, paprika Huhn Franz Lehar, sacher torte. *LD OPEN to 23.00. CLOSED Sat L, Sun.* **££**.

Tiroler Hut
27 Westbourne Grove W2. 01-727 3981. Tyrolean atmosphere with waitresses in national dress. Dancing, yodelling. Good value and excellent cooking. Leberknodel suppe, jagerschnitzel and apfel strudel. *D OPEN to 00.30. CLOSED Mon.* A. Ax. Dc. **£**.

Greek
Many Greek restaurants are run by Cypriots who have absorbed the best of both Greek and Turkish dishes into their style of cooking.

Boetys
79 St Martins Lane WC2. 01-836 8768. Comfortable establishment with authentic Greek cooking. Taramasalata, dolmadakia, arnaki. *OPEN to 23.30. CLOSED Sun.* A. Ax. B. Dc. E. **££.**

Blue Dolphin
40 Goodge St W1. 01-636 4874. Simple Greek restaurant. Charcoal grilled meats and kebabs, humous, kakoretsi and salad. Good Greek wine and coffee. *LD OPEN to 00.45. CLOSED Sun L.* **£.**

Hellenic
30 Thayer St W1. 01-935 1257. Genuine inexpensive Greco-Turkish food. Fried mussels with garlic, suckling pig, loukomades. *LD Reserve. OPEN to 23.30. CLOSED Sun.* **£.**

Kalamaras Taverna
76 Inverness Mews W2. 01-727 9122. True taverna atmosphere. Bouzouki players. Superb national dishes ranging from dolmades to baklava. *D Reserve. OPEN to 24.00. CLOSED Sun.* Ax.Dc. Children. **££.**

Trojan Horse
3 Milner St SW3. 01-589 4665. Excellent Greek-Cypriot food in Chelsea atmosphere. Humous, avgolemono, psito, moussaka. Bouzouki music. *D OPEN to 22.45. CLOSED Sun.* **£.**

White Tower
1 Percy St W1. 01-636 8141. Elegant; first class cuisine. Agreeable and leisurely service. Lemon soup, moussaka, dolmades. *LD Reserve. OPEN to 22.30. CLOSED Sat & Sun.* **£££.**

Hungarian
Hungarian food is distinguished by unusual but extremely tasty dishes. Fish are all of the freshwater variety. Carp and pike are presented in an impeccable style.

Gay Hussar
2 Greek St W1. 01-437 0973. Excellent Austro-Hungarian cooking. Good, enthusiastic service. Cold wild cherry soup, bulgar salata, roast partridge with lentils. *LD Reserve. OPEN to 23.30. CLOSED Sun & B. Hols.* **££.**

Le Mignon
2 Queensway W2. 01-229 0093. Typical Hungarian food, cheerful atmosphere and live gipsy orchestra. House sulz, chicken hongroise, fantanyeros, goulash. *LD OPEN to 24.00. CLOSED Mon.* **£.**

Indian
The farther south in India the hotter the spices. Madras, Bendi and Vindaloo mean climbing degrees of heat. For the European however there is no particular virtue in an excess of hotness — many Indians also enjoy (and prefer) mild curries. Hindu cooking uses vegetables in rich liquid juices; Muslims use more meat and the food is drier. The best cooking uses the traditional mud oven and adds spices individually to each dish, giving a distinctive and piquant flavour.

The Ganges One
40 Gerrard St W1. 01-387 0284. Specialises in authentic Indo-Pakistani dishes — some are newly introduced and unobtainable elsewhere. Tandoori dishes (baked in a clay oven) and tikkas. Indian music. *LD Reserve. OPEN to 23.00. Closed Sun.* A. Ax. B. Dc. Children. **£.**

The Gaylord
79 Mortimer St W1. 01-636 9802. Authentic Punjabi food. Spices added individually to each dish giving some delectable flavours. Tandoori chicken, lentils in cream and interesting Indian sweetmeats. *LD OPEN to 23.30.* A. Ax. B. Dc. E. **£.**

Shafi
18 Gerrard St W1. 01-437 2354. The oldest Indian restaurant in London. Some original dishes not found elsewhere. Samosas, chicken cucu-paka, potato chops. *LD OPEN to 23.30. CLOSED Sun* A. Ax. B. Cb. Dc. E. **£.**

Tandoori
153 Fulham Rd SW3. 01-589 7749. North-west frontier cooking of very high quality by Pathan chefs in the traditional clay ovens. Pleasant décor with soft music. Tandoori chicken, kebab, roghan josh. *D OPEN to 00.30. Sun L to 15.00.* A. Ax. B. Cb. Dc. E. **££.**

Veeraswamy's
99-101 Regent St (entrance in Swallow St) W1. 01-734 1401.. Authentic food in 'Indian Empire' atmosphere. Moglai, Delhi, Madras, Ceylon and Vindaloo curries. *LD OPEN to 23.00. Sun to 22.00.* A. Ax. B. Dc. Cb. E. **££.**

Italian
The largest group of foreign restaurants in London. One can eat cheaply or expensively and almost always get good food. These are some of the best:

Bertorelli's
19 Charlotte St W1. 01-636 4174
70-72 Queensway W2. 01-229 3160.
Busy straightforward Italian eating places. Good food at reasonable prices. Scampi, veal cutlet royal, filets de sole Bertorelli, zabaglioni. *LD OPEN to 22.00. CLOSED Sun & B Hols.* **££.**

Borgo Santa Croce
112 Cheyne Walk SW10. 01-352 7534. A branch of San Frediano's. Spacious, friendly trattoria with an original menu. Fresh salmon pâté en croûte, crespoline florentina, venison steaks. *LD Reserve. OPEN to 23.30. CLOSED Sun.* A. Ax. B. Dc. E. **££.**

La Capannina
24 Romilly St W1. 01-437 2473. Popular typical Soho trattoria. Music in the evening. Petto di pollo, vitello alla pianni. *LD Reserve. OPEN to 23.30.* Ax. B. Dc. **££.**

Gondoliere
3 Gloucester Rd SW7. 01-584 8062. Food served by Venetian gondoliers. Welcoming, restful atmosphere. Authentic cooking. Cartoccio del gondoliere, Dover Sole del gondoliere. *LD OPEN to 23.30. CLOSED Sat L & Sun.* Ax. B. Dc. Bank Americard. **££.**

Hostaria Romana
70 Dean St W1. 01-734 2869. Boisterous and busy, consistently good Roman cuisine. Regularly changed menu. Crespoline alla Romana, agnellino al forno, torta mela. *LD Reserve. OPEN to 23.30.* A. Ax. Cb. E. **£.**

Medusa
38c Kensington Church St W8. 01-937 2005. Good pasta dishes, penne a la carbonara, rack of lamb with herbs and white wine. *LD Reserve. OPEN to 24.00. CLOSED Sun.* A. Ax. B. Dc. E. **££.**

Mimmo d'Ischia
61 Elizabeth St SW1. 01-730 5406. Intimate, comfortable and busy. Original and imaginative dishes. Good spigola and spare ribs Casanova. *LD Reserve. OPEN to 23.45. CLOSED Sun.* A. Ax. B. Dc. **££.**

Peter Mario
47 Gerrard St W1. 01-437 4170. Carefully cooked food in a friendly setting. Generous helpings. Excellent soups, scaloppini Peter Mario. *LD OPEN to 23.30. CLOSED Sun.* A. Ax. B. Dc. E. **££.**

San Frediano
62 Fulham Rd SW3. 01-584 8375. Bright and lively trattoria with friendly service. Excellent Italian dishes, particularly good fish and a tempting sweet trolley, all at reasonable prices. Clam salad, scallopino uccellato. *LD Reserve. OPEN to 23.30. CLOSED Sun.* A. Ax. B. Dc. E. **££.**

San Lorenzo
22 Beauchamp Place SW3. 01-584 1074. Very popular and friendly restaurant offering a different menu every day. *LD OPEN to 23.30. CLOSED Sun.* **££.**

Tiberio
22 Queen St W1. 01-629 3561. Top-quality Roman cooking in popular, crowded atmosphere. Band for

dancing. *23.30-02.00*. Tripe 'Petronius', fettucine alla panna, duck and quail. *LD Reserve. OPEN to 01.30. CLOSED L Sat & Sun*. A. Ax. B. Cb. Dc. E. **£££.**

Japanese

Ginnan
5 Cathedral Place EC4. 01-236 4120. Crowded; polite and efficient service. Raw fish sachimi, excellent soups, soba and domburi dishes. Food fried in front of you. Traditional Tempura (deep fried sea food with subtle sauces). *LD Reserve. OPEN to 22.00. CLOSED Sat & Sun*. **££.**

Hiroko
6-8 St Christopher's Place W1. 01-935 1579. The first authentic Japanese restaurant in London. Service by graceful and charming Japanese girls in kimonos. Completely oriental atmosphere. Try the complete dinner, Sukiyaki or Tempura. Saké or Japanese beer. *LD OPEN to 22.30. CLOSED Sun*. Ax. B. Cb. Dc. E. **££.**

Hokkai
61 Brewer St W1. 01-734 5826. Japanese prints and red lanterns. Traditional dishes. *LD Reserve. OPEN to 23.00. CLOSED Sun L*. A. Ax. B. Dc. E. **££.**

Jewish

Bloom's
90 Whitechapel High St F1. 01-247 6001.
130 Golders Green Rd NW11. 01-455 1338.
Authentic Kosher restaurants. Busy and popular. Probably the best Jewish cooking in London. Large helpings; lockshen and meat balls, salt beef, stuffed kishka. *LD Open to 21.30. CLOSED Fri from 15.00, Sat & Jewish hols. OPEN B. Hols*. **£.**

Goody's Original Kosher Restaurant
55 Berwick St W1. 01-437 6050. 60 year old Kosher restaurant of good value. Comfortable and friendly. Generous helpings. Braten (braised beef) and lockshen pudding. *LD Reserve. OPEN to 22.00*. A. Ax. B. Dc. Cb. E. **££.**

Polish and Russian

Luba's Bistro
6 Yeoman's Row SW3. 01-589 2950. Individual, down to earth spartan atmosphere. Good peasant-style cooking at low prices. Borscht, beef Stroganoff, shashlik, pojarsky. *LD OPEN to 24.00. CLOSED Sun*. **£.**

Nikita's
65 Ifield Rd SW10. 01-352 6326. Russian dishes, slightly adapted to Western tastes. Small basement restaurant, quite pretty. Selection of vodka. *D OPEN to 23.30. CLOSED Sun. B. Dc*. **£££.**

Portuguese

O Fado
50 Beauchamp Place, SW1. 01-589 3002. A genuine Portuguese restaurant with music in the basement. Sardines and the chicken speciality, franguintos a Fado, are superb. Good carafe wine. *D OPEN to 24.30, Sun to 23.30.* E. **£.**

Scandinavian

Hungry Viking
44 Ossington St W2. 01-727 3311. All the food here is home-made and includes pâtés, marinated herring and the traditional Smorgasbord. Good hot dish of the day. *D Reserve. OPEN to 23.00. CLOSED Mon.* Ax. B. Dc. **££.**

Norway Food Centre
166 Brompton Rd SW3. 01-584 6062. Smorgasbord, cold table of fish and meats and some hot dishes. Help yourself from a vast selection of delicacies assisted by attractive girls in national costume. Norwegian beer or akvavit. *LD Reserve. OPEN to 22.30. CLOSED Sun L. Children.* **££.**

Spanish & Mexican

El Bodegon
9 Park Walk SW10. 01-352 1330. Intimate, cool and popular. Mainly Spanish dishes, excellently cooked. Gambas al pil-pil, pechuga de pollo noche de gala (stuffed chicken breasts in raisins and champagne), trenera sacromonte. *LD Reserve. OPEN to 23.30.* A. Ax. B. Dc. E. **££.**

La Cucaracha
12-13 Greek St W1. 01-734 2253. London's first Mexican restaurant, in the cellars of a converted monastery. Raw fish cocktail, arroz à la poblana, enchiladas. Spicy and delicious. *LD OPEN to 23.30. CLOSED Sat L & Sun.* A. Ax. b. Cb. Dc. E. **££.**

Martinez
25 Swallow St W1. 01-734 5066. Old-fashioned, beautifully decorated Spanish-style restaurant. Courteous service; guitarist. Gazpacho, paella Valencia, good tortillas. *LD Reserve. OPEN to 23.30. Sun to 22.30.* A. Ax. B. Dc. E. **££.**

La Parra
163 Draycott Avenue SW3. 01 589 2913. Good Spanish and Latin American dishes. Gazpacho, gambas pil-pil, Basque crab, chicken Marrakesh. *D. Reserve. OPEN to 23.00. CLOSED Sun.* Ax. B. Dc. E. **££.**

Swiss

The Swiss Centre

1 New Coventry St (Leicester Square) W1. 01-734 1291. Four different restaurants of varying prices, of which the Taverne seems the most popular. Imaginative decoration. Fondue, Swiss country hams, pasta and delicious pastries. *LD OPEN to 24.00.* A. Ax. B. Dc.

Turkish

Adana Kebab Centre

17 Colomb St SE10. 01-858 1913. Busy, thriving Turkish restaurant with excellent Mediterranean foods. Chicken with lemon and bay leaves, humous, yogurtlu. Drink retsina or buzbag. *D. Reserve. OPEN to 24.00. CLOSED Sun. Dc.* **£.**

Gallipoli

8 Bishopsgate Churchyard EC2. 01-588 1922. Once a Turkish bath, with original gold décor and tiles; now an exotic restaurant with plump belly dancers. Excellent Turkish food. 20-dish hors d'oeuvre, shashlik and kebabs. Two shows nightly *22.00 and 01.00. LD Reserve. OPEN to 03.00. CLOSED Sun.* A. Ax. B. Cb. Dc. E. **£££.**

Nibub Lokanta

112 Edgware Rd W2. 01-262 6636. Fairly authentic Turkish dishes, usually tasty. Good variety of kebabs. Karisik mezze, kuzu but (lamb fillets) and plenty of yoghourt dishes. *LD Reserve. OPEN to 23.30.* A. Ax. B. Dc. E. **££.**

Vegetarian and health food

These places serve mainly salads, omelettes and savouries. Some people eat in them for religious reasons, others because it's healthy and less fattening.

Cranks

William Blake House, Marshall St W1. 01-427 9431. Modern, attractive décor; background of classical music. Home-made soups, hot vegetable savoury, mixed salads with fruit and nuts, good cheeses and sweets, and bread from their own bakery. *OPEN to 20.30, Sat to 16.30. CLOSED Sun.* **£.**

Also branch in Heal's, Tottenham Court Rd W1. 01-636 2230. *OPEN Mon-Sat 10.00-17.00.* **£.**

Food for Health Restaurants

15 Blackfriars Lane EC4. 01-236 7001.
85 Blomfield House, London Wall EC2. 01-588 3446. Lunches only. Seven different fresh salads, omlettes, soufflés and savouries. Crowded. *OPEN 08.30-15.30. CLOSED Sat & Sun.* **£.**

Food for Thought
31 Neal St WC2. 01-836 0239. Vegetarian wholefood in a cheerful Covent Garden basement. Occasional 'music and poetry evenings'. *LD OPEN to 20.00. CLOSED Sun.* **£.**

Nuthouse
26 Kingly St W1. 01-437 9471. Buffet service vegetarian health food on two floors. Nut roasts, quiches, blackberry pie, fresh raspberry juice. *LD OPEN to 20.00. CLOSED Sat & Sun.* **£.**

Oodles
31 Cathedral Place EC4. 01-248 2559.
3 Fetter Lane EC4. 01-353 1984.
14 Fulwood Place WC1. 01-242 6165.
113 High Holborn WC1. 01-204 3838.
42 New Oxford St WC1. 01-580 3762.
Very popular; clean scrubbed tables. Well-balanced salads and savoury foods. Generous hot dishes. *OPEN 10.30-18.00. CLOSED Sun.* **£.**

Sharuna Restaurant
107 Great Russell St WC1. 01-636 5922. An elegant South-Indian vegetarian restaurant. The highest quality and cleanliness. Vegetarian curries, delicately spiced, yogurt and fruit. *LD OPEN to 21.45. Sun 13.00-21.00.* **£.**

Fish

Fish and chips is a national dish which you take away with vinegar, salt and pepper. Eaten hot it can be delicious and good value. (The following restaurants are not fish and chip shops.)

Bentley's
11-15 Swallow St W1. 01-734 6210. Famous seafood restaurant and oyster bar. Lobster Newburg, sole meunière, prawns, crabs and fish of many sorts. *LD Reserve. OPEN to 22.45. CLOSED Sun.* A. Ax. B. Cb. Dc. E. **££.**

Geale's
2 Farmer St W8. 01-727 7969. Going since 1919, this is fish and chips with a difference. Cod's roe, scampi, sole, trout, skate delivered fresh daily. Soup, fruit salad and, surprisingly, a wine list (featuring champagne!) *LD OPEN to 22.45. CLOSED Sun & Mon.* **£.**

Overton's
5 St James's St SW1. 01-839 3774. Long-established fish restaurant of character. 'Old world' atmosphere in the nicest sense. Oysters, lobsters, Dover sole. *LD Reserve. OPEN to 23.00. CLOSED Sun.* A. Ax. b. Dc. E. **£££.**

Sheekey's
28-32 St Martin's Court WC2. 01-836 4118. Family-owned since 1896. Fresh salmon, steamed turbot with lobster sauce, stewed eels. Crowded. *LD OPEN to 20.30. CLOSED Sun, D Sat*. A. Ax. B. Dc. **££**.

Sweeting's
39 Queen Victoria St EC2. 01-248 3062. Echo of a vanished age. Fish parlour, with excellent service. Sit at the bar and eat herrings with mustard, whitebait, fish pie of excellent quality. Good carafe and port. *L OPEN to 15.00. CLOSED Sat, Sun*. **£**.

Wheeler's Fish restaurants
Alcove
17 Kensington High St W8. 01-937 1443. As in all Wheeler's restaurants, only fresh ingredients of high quality are used in the preparation of fish dishes; whitebait, sole bonne femme, prawn thermidor. *LD Reserve. OPEN to 23.00. CLOSED Sun*. A. Ax. B. Cb. Dc. **£££**.

Antoine
40 Charlotte St W1. 01-636 2817. Small restaurant on 3 floors specialising in sea food. Lobster, smoked salmon, moules marinière and many ways of serving sole and halibut. *LD Reserve. OPEN to 23.00*. A. Ax. B. D. Cb. **£££**.

George & Dragon
256 Brompton Rd SW3. 01-584 2626. *LD Reserve. OPEN to 23.00*. A. Ax. B. Cb. Dc. **£££**.

Wheeler's
19 Old Compton St W1. 01-437 2706. *LD Reserve. OPEN to 23.00*. A. Ax. B. Cb. Dc. **£££**.

Inexpensive eating

Places where you can eat well for under £3.00 (in some cases under £1.00). The café serving 'sausage, egg and chips' is not included here, however excellent some may be. This list prizes distinctive or unusual cooking and atmosphere — but particularly good value for money.

Al Ristoro
205 Kensington Church St W8. 01-727 3184. Genuine very good value Italian food. Canelloni, saltimbocca Romana. Italian ices. *LD OPEN to 23.30. CLOSED L Sun*. **£**.

Alpino restaurants
43 New Oxford St WC1. 01-836 1011.
29 Leicester Square WC2. 01-839 2939.
102 Wigmore St W1. 01-935 4181.
Busy and popular with Italian atmosphere. Service efficient and quick. Good selection of Alpine dishes. *LD OPEN to 23.30. CLOSED Sun*. A. Ax. B. Dc. **£**.

Ceylon Tea Centre
22 Regent St SW1. 01-930 8632. Good, varied and unusual salads, savouries and cheese flans. The different sorts of tea are first class. *L OPEN to 18.00. CLOSED Sun.* **£.**

Chelsea Kitchen
98 Kings Rd SW3. 01-589 1330. Part of the Stockpot group. The daily menu offers a good choice of hot cheap dishes. Soup, moussaka, spaghetti, ice cream and hot chocolate sauce. *LD OPEN to 24.00.* **£.**

Daquise
20 Thurloe St SW7. 01-589 6117. Simple, very cheap Polish food. Pierozki, shashlik, bitok. Many Polish customers. *LD OPEN to 23.45.* **£.**

Great American Disaster
9 Beauchamp Place SW3. 01-589 0992. Very popular. Hamburgers and traditional American fare . Several branches. *LD OPEN to 24.00, Sat & Sun to 01.00.* **£.**

Hamburger Products
1 Brewer St W1. 01-437 7119. Small fish bar. Cockney atmosphere. All fish freshly caught and home smoked. Smoked eel with pepper salad . Trout with beetroot salad 63p. *L OPEN to 15.00. CLOSED Sat & Sun.* **£.**

Hard Rock Café
150 Old Park Lane W1. 01-629 0382. One of the best hamburger places in London with relaxed, colourful atmosphere. Check tablecloths, wooden tables, rock music. A shorts bar and good hamburgers, sandwiches and steaks. Schlitz beer. *LD OPEN to 00.30.* **£.**

Jimmy's
24 Frith St W1. 01-437 9521. Crowded Turkish basement restaurant, very popular with students. Large helpings of meat, greens and haricot beans plus fresh salad and as much bread as you want. *LD OPEN to 22.00.* A. Ax. B. Dc. **£.**

Pizza Express
30 Coptic St WC1. 01-636 3232. Modern pizza parlour with a large red pizza oven in the middle. Many varieties. Good ice creams. Many branches. *LD OPEN to 24.00.* **£.**

Romano Santi
50 Greek St W1. 01-437 2350. The set lunch is probably the finest value in London. Also excellent set dinner. *LD OPEN to 23.30. CLOSED Sun.* A. Ax. B. Dc. E. **£.**

Spaghetti House
15-17 Goodge St W1. 01-636 6582. Very busy, friendly restaurant. Separate kitchens on all three floors. Reasonably priced. Very good pastas and spaghettis. Cervella di vitello Milanese, saltimbocca alla Romana. Many branches. *LD OPEN to 23.00. CLOSED Sun.* **£.**

Outdoor eating

The continental habit of eating outside can be very pleasant on a hot summer's day. The following places have a few tables on the pavement or in the garden. There are also several in Charlotte St and Wigmore St W1.

Anemos
34 Charlotte St W1. 01-580 5907. Friendly, crowded and noisy, with customers and waiters singing and dancing on the tables. Eat outside at the pavement tables in summer. Humous, excellent kebabs, moussaka. *LD OPEN to 24.00. CLOSED Sun.* **£.**

Au Bon Accueil
27 Elystan St SW3. 01-589 3718. Tables set out on the pavement in summer. Comfortable French restaurant with excellent cuisine. Escalope au rhum et orange, filet mignon sauce béarnaise. *LD Reserve. OPEN to 23.30. CLOSED Sat L & Sun.* A. Ax. Dc. **£.**

Froops
17 Princess Rd NW1. 01-722 9663. Bistro restaurant with a proper garden, partially covered and very full in summer. French provincial and 'Franglais' dishes. *D Reserve. OPEN to 23.30. CLOSED Sun.* Ax. B. Dc. **££.**

The Rose Garden
Queen Mary's Rose Garden, Regent's Park NW1. 01-935 5729. Open-air eating in a London park at tables with parasols. Unadventurous English food. *LD OPEN To 23.00 in summer, to 18.00 in winter.* A. Ax. B. Dc. **£.** *Cafeteria open to 19.00.*

San Lorenzo Fuoriporta
Worple Road Mews SW19. 01-946 8463. Cheerful, lively trattoria with tables in the garden during summer. Play boules in the courtyard; an ideal spot for Sunday lunches with children. Scalloppine di vitello alla San Lorenzo petti di pollo, good fresh vegetables. *LD Reserve. OPEN to 23.30.* A. Ax B. Dc. E. **££.**

Unusual eating

Beachcomber (Polynesian)
Mayfair Hotel, Berkeley St W1. 01-629 7777. Hawaii and the South Seas, complete with alligators and tropical atmosphere. Chinese and Polynesian food. Polynesian pâté, chicken momi, steak luau. *D Reserve. OPEN to 23.30. Dancing 20.30-02.00. CLOSED Sun.* **££.**

Dizzy's Diner (Victorian fantasy)
25 Basil St SW3. 01-589 8444. All in honour of Benjamin Disraeli. Victorian styled eating place. Not expensive. *LD OPEN to 23.30.* A. Ax. B. Dc. **£.**

1520 A.D. (Mediaeval Banquets)
St Martin's Lane WC2. 01-240 3978. Jesters and troubadours entertain while you eat your 7-course meal. Specialities include old English beef, not roast but stewed. *D Reserve. OPEN to 24.00.* A. Ax. B. Cb. Dc. E. **££.**

Flanagan's (Victorian Fantasy)
100 Baker St W1. 01-935 0287.
37 St Martin's Lane WC2. 01-836 5358.
Completely phoney (but enjoyable) Victorian 'dining rooms', with sawdust for spitting on, stalls, cockney songs and colourful signs, notices and extravaganza. Elegantly costumed waiters and serving girls (usually pleasantly independent Aussies). Tripe, jellied eels, game pie, enormous plates of fish and chips, golden syrup pudding. *LD OPEN to 23.15.* A. Ax. B. Cb. Dc. E. **£.**

Gallipoli (Belly dancers)
8 Bishopsgate Churchyard EC2. 01-588 1922. Exotic and unusual. Twice nightly cabaret of enjoyable and erotic Eastern belly dancing. Excellent Turkish food. Shish kebab, buryan Gallipoli, red mullet. *LD Reserve. OPEN to 03.00. CLOSED Sun. Cabaret 22.30-01.00.* A. Ax. B. Cb. Dc. E. **£££.**

Hispaniola (Dinner afloat)
The Thames at Victoria Embankment, Charing Cross WC2. 01-839 3011. A restaurant floating on the Thames. Romantic setting. Good Spanish food on upper or lower deck. *LD Reserve. OPEN to 23.20, Sun to 21.50.* A. Ax. B. Dc. **£££.**

Trader Vic's (South Seas)
London Hilton, 22 Park Lane W1. 01-493 8000. Atmosphere of Pacific Islands and the Orient in décor and food. South sea drinks. Tahitian fish soup, duckling barbecued, quenelles de Mahi Mahi. *LD OPEN to 23.45. CLOSED L Sat.* A. Ax. B. Dc. E. **££.**

London's famous pubs

Most London pubs date back to the 19th cent but many are up to 400 years old. Some take on the character and needs of the locality and are aptly called 'locals' while others provide cheerful places to relax for workers, shoppers or theatre-goers. Of the 1,000 pubs in London we have selected some of the most interesting, but there are many more to be discovered by the thirsty or the curious.
Open hours vary but usually 11.00-15.00 and 17.30-23.00 with earlier closing on Sun.

L-*lunch;* **D**-*dinner;* **B**-*buffet. Most pubs serve snacks, some have hot buffet lunches and many have restaurants. These are indicated in the following list.*

Bitter
The most popular beer which comes in two grades; ordinary and best. On draught or from the keg, the latter is the most expensive. All English beers are served at cellar temperature and are best savoured that way.

Mild
The least strong as its name implies.

Mixed
Half a pint of bitter mixed with half a pint of mild.

Stout
A very dark bottled beer. Guinness is the most popular variety and can be obtained on draught.

Barley wine
A very potent bottled drink equivalent in effect to a double whiskey and much cheaper.

Lager
The nearest equivalent to the Continental beers. Usually served chilled on draught or bottled.

Cider
Rough cider on draught is hard to come by; bottled cider is sweeter.

Shandy
Can be bought made with equal amounts of bitter and lemonade, or bottled.

Light or Pale Ale
Bottled beer.

Brown Ale
Sweet dark bottled beer.

Ginger beer
Non-alcoholic fizzy drink, often used in shandy instead of lemonade.

Baker and Oven
10 Paddington St W1. 01-935 5072. Small colourful orange and green pub with cosy basement alcoves and bars. Mouth watering home-made pies from 100 year old baker's ovens. **B D**

Black Friar
174 Queen Victoria St EC4. 01-236 5650. Triangular building in the shadows of Blackfriars railway bridge. Stunning shades of Art Nouveau mixed with Gothic; excellent buffet if you can get your eyes off the decor. **B**

Bunch of Grapes
207 Brompton Rd SW3. 01-589 4944. Popular Victorian pub with finely engraved 'snob-screens' separating the bars and impressively carved wooden pillars. **B**

Cheshire Cheese, Ye Olde
145 Fleet St EC4. 01-353 6170. Rebuilt after the Great Fire with low ceiling'd interiors, oak tables, sawdust on the floor. The pub probably hasn't changed much since Dr Johnson used to drop in. No snacks but good traditional English cooking for those in search of a meal.

Dirty Dick's
202-4 Bishopsgate EC2. 01-283 5888. The original pub named after Nat Bentley, well known 18th cent miser of the ballad. Lives up to its name with cobwebs and musty stuffed cats. **B D**

George Inn
77 Borough High St SE1. 01-407 2056. Galleried Dickensian coaching inn mentioned in 'Little Dorrit'. Excellent beer, dispensed from an unusual 'beer engine', mussels, sprats, cockles and jellied eels. **B C**

Gilbert and Sullivan
John Adam St WC2. 01-839 2580. Strictly a G & S lovers pub. Programmes, playbills, photographs, scores and stage settings — and of course the music. **B D**

Hole in the Wall
5 Mepham St SE1. 01-407 1204. Free house. Bass Worthington, Brakspear Ruddle County and Young's cask bitters. Built into the arches by Waterloo Station with bar-loads of beer fanatics.

Lamb and Flag
33 Rose, St Covent Garden WC2. 01-836 4108. Originally called 'The Bucket of Blood' because the pub was the centre for fighting in the area (Dryden apparently got the 'once over' here). Now a popular mellow bar. **B**

Museum Tavern
49 Great Russell St WC1. 01-242 8987. Located opposite the British Museum, the tavern attracts students and sightseers. Victorian interior with a vast collection of bowler hats and umbrellas! **B**

Nag's Head
79-81 Heath St NW3. 01-435 4108. Crowded every night with dedicated beer swillers sampling the impressive selection offered. Small patio. **B**

Orange
37 Pimlico Rd SW1. 01-730 5378. Nell Gwyn once sold oranges here. Cheerful atmosphere. **B**

Printer's Devil
98 Fetter Lane EC4. 01-242 2239. A printers' and journalists' pub named after the traditional printers' apprentice. Notable collection of early printing curios. **B**

Sherlock Holmes
10 Northumberland St WC2. 01-930 2644. Perfect replica of Holmes' study at 221b Baker St. **B D**

Musical pubs

Bull's Head
Barnes Bridge SW13. 01-876 5241. Modern jazz by top
English and visiting foreign players *every night.*
Greyhound
175 Fulham Palace Rd W6. 01-385 0526. *Every night.*
Excellent value with no entrance fee.
Hope and Anchor
207 Upper St N1. 01-359 4510. Beery pub with loud juke
box upstairs, live music in the cellar *Mon-Sat* nights.
Good food and open fires in winter.
King's Head
115 Upper St N1. 01-226 1916. Live music *every night*
from skiffle bands to trad jazz. Rock *at weekends.* **D**
Mathilda's
Old Swan, 206 Kensington Church St W8. 01-229 8421.
Every night with singers and musicians welcome. All
sorts of folk ranging from Aussie and blue grass to old
time. Free.
New Merlin's Cave
Margery St WC1. 01-837 2097. Barn-like pub offering
jazz *Wed-Fri,* and good *Sun lunchtime* sessions. Top
musicians drop in and play gratis.
Pindar of Wakefield
328 Gray's Inn Rd WC1. 01-837 7269. The pub to go to
for oldtime music-hall. *Thur, Fri & Sat nights* — book
first for an excellent show. **B**
Plough
90 Stockwell Rd SW9. 01-274 3879. Top quality jazz.
Different groups *Wed-Sun.*
Prospect of Whitby
57 Wapping Wall E1. 01-481 1095. 600 year old Pepys
tavern overlooking the Thames. Nautical souvenirs and
excellent restaurant with balcony. Jazz *Tues-Sun.*
Queens Head
83 Fieldgate St E1. 01-247 5593. Free and easy East End
pub. Seamen and vodka. Oldtime piano music.
The Rising Sun, Granny's Folk Blues Club
46 Tottenham Court Rd W1. 01-636 6530. Friendly and
informal. Singers welcome. *Fri & Sat.*
Two Brewers
40 Monmouth St WC2. 01-836 7395. Warm and friendly
oak-panelled pub with strong local following. Renowned
jazz jam sessions *Mon & Fri.* A *must* for enthusiasts. **B.**
White Hart
191 Drury Lane WC2. 01-405 4061. Another pub that
claims to be the oldest in London. Friendly and loud
with jazz *every night* — mainly trad.

Drag pubs
Female impersonators enjoy an enormous popularity in pubs with acts that are a combination of blue jokes and songs. There is usually a central roster of artistes who do the round of these better known pubs:

Black Cap
171 Camden High St NW1. 01-485 1742. *Every night.*

Elephant and Castle
2 South Lambeth Place SW8. 01-735 1001. *Every night.* Also live bands.

King's Head
48 Gerrard St W1. 01-437 5858. Drag shows *on Sat & Sun* in one of the oldest Dive Bars in London.

Royal Vauxhall Tavern
372 Kennington Lane SE11. 01-582 0833. *Every night.*

Union Tavern
146 Camberwell New Rd SE5. 01-735 3605. Revues on *Tues, Wed, Thur and Sun* in one of London's original drag pubs. House band on *Fri & Sat.*

Open air pubs
Where you can enjoy a drink outside — on a pavement, in a courtyard or garden, or overlooking the river.

Anchor
Bankside SE1. 01-407 1577. 18th cent replacement of original destroyed by fire of 1676. Five beamed bars and three restaurants — one with a minstrel's gallery. **B D**

The Crown
35 Albert Embankment SW1. 01-735 1054. Lovely view over the river to the Houses of Parliament. **B**

Flask
77 West Hill, Highgate N6. 01-340 3969. Old tavern named after the flasks which people used to buy here to fill with water at the Hampstead wells. Crowded forecourt for outside drinking.

Grapes
76 Narrow St, Limehouse E14. 01-987 4396. Traditional pub amid wharves and warehouses. **B**

Mayflower
117 Rotherhithe St SE16. 01-237 4088. Tudor Thames-side inn connected historically with the Pilgrim Fathers. Good grills. **B D**

Old Caledonia
Victoria Embankment (under Waterloo Bridge) WC2. 01-240 2750. An old converted paddle-steamer. Ideal for a hot summer's evening, but if you've got a queasy stomach, then pray for no wind! **B D**

Spaniards Inn
Hampstead Lane NW3. 01-455 3276. Famous 16th cent inn with Dick Turpin and literary associations. Beer garden. **B**

SHOPPING

London is one of the world's finest shopping centres, with a wonderful balance of luxury and utility shops; huge department stores and intimate boutiques; market stalls selling anything and everything and expensive specialist shops.

Shopping hours

Most shops in central London open at 09.30 hrs on weekdays, and stay open until 17.30 hrs. Some close early on Sat (13.00) but have one late-night opening during the week, usually on Thursday till 19.00 hrs. Shops in the suburbs stay open all day Sat, but have one early closing day in the week, nearly all the shops in that district will be closed for that afternoon.

Tourist Concessions

Most of the large department stores have Export Bureaux which will arrange for your purchases to be sent abroad, free of Value Added Tax. If you buy over the counter though, you will have to pay the full amount and arrange to receive a refund later. Common Market visitors exceeding their allowances may be subject to customs duty on their return, but the stores are familiar with the regulations and will advise you.

Souvenirs

All goods manufactured in England are the best buys. Dress and furnishing fabrics, particularly tweeds, cashmeres and woollens are of excellent quality and well worth the money. The ready-to-wear clothes in London rival those produced anywhere in the world in price, quality and design, so anything you buy in this line is likely to be a bargain. Other worthwhile purchases are leather goods — coats, shoes and accessories; china, particularly Wedgwood and porcelain; silver and antiques, rare books and prints. There are many shops geared for the tourist, with plastic beafeaters etc. and almost everything has a Union Jack on it!

Markets

Markets are a colourful and vital part of London's trade and everyday life. These are the best known, although there are literally hundreds of smaller street markets in the suburbs. They are still tremendously popular, despite the growing number of supermarkets and offer every kind of article for household use.

Berwick Street
Soho W1. It's worth braving the aggressive stall-holders: the fruit and vegetables are good, and prices reasonable, particularly at the southern end of the street. *Mon-Sat 08.00-19.00.*

Camden Lock
Where Chalk Farm Rd crosses Regent's Canal NW6. Small antique, junk and bric-a-brac market. Also art and craft shops set in a cobbled courtyard beside the pretty lock and canal walks. Good hot food stand by the entrance. *Sat & Sun 08.00-18.00.*

Camden Passage
Islington High St N1. A paved walk lined with a mixture of shops and stalls; the haunt of the trendies, selling a mixture of antiques and attractive, but expensive, bric-a-brac. Particulary fine art-deco shop and opposite, a print shop which repays frequent visiting. *Mon-Sat 09.00-18.00.*

Chelsea Antiques Market
253 Kings Rd SW3. Large confused market spreading back from the Kings Rd. Mostly general stock, but some specialists. Worth including on a visit to the area.

Leadenhall Market
Gracechurch St EC3. General retail market: vegetables, poultry, plants, fish and endless other items. The late Victorian glass and ironwork of the building is superb. *Mon-Fri 09.00-17.00. Shellfish on Sun.*

Petticoat Lane
Radiates from Middlesex St E1. Huge bustling complex selling everything under the sun; some bargains, lots of rubbish but, most important, an atmosphere of fun. Some of the streets leading off the main road of stalls specialise in one type of thing e.g. **Club Row** deals in fish, birds, reptiles and mammals while neighbouring **Brick Lane** is good for furniture and electrical equipment. *Sun only.*

Portobello Road
Nr Notting Hill Gate tube W11. Superb flea-market, though now too well known for many bargains to exist. Vegetables, fruit and flowers *Mon-Sat 07.00-18.00* plus antiques, bizarre clothes and a welter of glorious junk on *Sat.*

Oxford street

	187	**Penberthy's** *Fashion F*

Great Titchfield street

Ramilles place

Shoes **Ravel**	184		**199**	**Zales** *Jewellers*
Turf accountant Ladbrokes	190		**201**	**Harlequin** *Records*
Shoes **Mr Henry**	192		**213**	**LITTLEWOODS** *STORE*
Restaurant Quality Inn	192			
Midland Bank	196		**217**	**Wallis** *Fashion F*
STORE **C & A**	202		**219**	**Ratners** *Jewellers*

Great Portland street

Hills place

Restaurant Café Torino	214		**221**	**Alexandre's** *Fashion M*
Fashion M **Peter Brown**	220		**225**	Studio One & Two *Cinemas*
Shoes **R P Ellen**	222		**225**	**Sacha** *Shoes F*
			231	**Jean Junction**
			231	**Jeans West**
			231	Lighter Repair Centre
			233	**Mr. Byrite** *Fashion M*
			235	Bank of Credit & Commerce

STORE **PETER ROBINSON**

Argyll street

	241	**Finlays** *Tobacconist*
	⊖	Oxford Circus
		Wedgwood Shop *China*
		Goldsmiths & Silversmiths Shop

Oxford circus

Regent street

Fashion M **John Collier**	240			South African Airways
Fashion F **Harper's House**	240		**257**	**Images** *Fashion F*
			259	**Jean Machine**
John Prince's street			**261**	**Zales** *Jewellers*
Travel agency Pontins	242		**263**	**Richard Shops** *Fashion F*
Shoes **Bally**	246		**267**	**Dorothy Perkins** *Fashion F*
Shoes **Ravel**	248		**271**	Reed *Employment agency*
Jewellers **H Samuel**	250		**273**	**Oxford Woollens** *Fabrics M*
STORE **BRITISH HOME STORES**	252		**275**	Rink Club
Shoes **Peter Lord**	260		**275**	Salvation Army Hall
Fashion Ch **Ladybird**	262		**277**	**Ernest Jones** *Jewellers*
Fashion F **Etam**	264		**283**	**Girl** *Fashion F*
Jewellers **Leslie Davis**	266		**285**	**Garb** *Fashion F*
JEAN MACHINE	268		**287**	**Bata** *Shoes*
Fashion F M **John Stephen**	268		**289**	Old Kentucky *Restaurant*
Fashion F **Wallis**	272		**291**	Brook Street *Employment agency*
			291a	**Snob** *Fashion F*
			291b	National Westminster Bank

Holles street

Harewood place

			293	**Saxone** *Shoes*
			299	**Babers** *Shoes*
STORE **JOHN LEWIS**			**299**	City Centre *Employment agency*
			299	Paris Academy Fashion School
			301	**Freeman Hardy & Willis** *Shoes*
			303	**Dolcis** *Shoes*
			309	**Berkertex** *Fashion F*
			311	**WOOLWORTHS** *STORE*
			313	**Ratners** *Jewellers*

Old Cavendish street

STORE **D H EVANS**		
	315	Acme *Employment agency*
	315	**Mates** *Fashion F M*

Chapel place

Dering street

K Shoes	324		**321**	Berlitz School of Languages
Regent Furs	326		**325**	**Lord John** *Fashion F M*
Jean Machine	328		**325**	**Mansfield** *Shoes*
Bank of Scotland	332			

Vere street

New Bond street

STORE **DEBENHAMS**			**333**	**Dolcis** *Shoes*
			335	**NW Souvenirs**
			337	**Jean Junction**
			337	**Sacha** *Shoes F*
			343	Indian Tea Centre *Restaurant*

Woodstock street

Shoes **Dolcis**	350		**351**	**Sacha** *Shoes F*
			353	**Dormeuil** *Fabrics M*
Marylebone lane			**353**	Brook Street *Employment agency*
			357	**Squire Shop** *Fashion M*
NW Souvenirs	354			
Fashion F M **Mates**	356		**Sedley place**	
National Westminster Bank	358		**359**	Railway Lost Property Office
			359	**Denise** *Fashion F*
			361	**Downtown** *Fashion F M*
			361	Find and Place *Employment agency*
			363	**His Masters Voice** *Records*
			369	**Angella** *Fashion F*
			369a	**David Leslie** *Jewellers*
			373	**Ratners** *Jewellers*

Stratford place

Davies street

Shoes **Lilley & Skinner**	360		⊖	Bond street
Fashion M **Take Six**	364		**385**	**Boots** *Chemist*
Fashion M **Michael Barrie**	366			
Fashion M **Lord John**	368		**393**	**Coles** *Fashion M*
Fashion F **Richard Shops**	372		**395**	**Everon** *Fashion F*

James street

Gilbert street

Left		Right	
STORE **C & A**	376	399	Garners Steak House *Restaurant*
		399	Lloyds Bank
Bird street			**Binney street**
Fashion F **Gilda**	386	407	British Rail Travel Office
Fashion F **Jane Norman**	388	409	**Jean Machine** *Fashion F M*
Shoes **Barratts**	388	411	**Woodhouse** *Fashion M*
		413	National Westminster Bank
			Duke street
		415	**Hornes** *Fashion M*
		419	**Burton & Top Shop** *Fashion F M*
			Lumley street
		421	Superama
		423	Jean Jeanie
		429	Wimpy Bar *Restaurant*
			Balderton street
STORE **SELFRIDGES**		431	Midland Bank
		435	**The Sheepskin Shop**
		439	**Thackerays** *Fashion M*
		439	Butlins Holiday Camps
		443	**Milletts** *Fashion F M & camping centre*
		447	**John Stephen** *Fashions F M*
		449	Instant Passport Photos
		449	**Athena Reproductions** *Posters & prints*
		451	Barclays Bank
Orchard street			**North Audley street**
STORE **MARKS & SPENCER**		455	Angus Steak House *Restaurant*
		461	**Mothercare** *Baby store*
National Westminster Bank	466	467	**Jean Machine**
Fashion F **Fairman**	470	469	**Dormeuil** *Tax Free Shop Fabrics M*
Shoes **Bally**	474	471	**Grand Woollen Centre** *Fabrics M & Tailor*
Jewellers **Herbert Wolf**	476	473	**Westerner** *Fashion MF*
Jewellers **Ratners**	478	475	**Hepworths** *Fashion M*
Fashion F **Richard Shops**	480	477	**Take Six** *Fashion M*
Fashion F **Etam**	484	479	Tennessee Pancake House *Restaurant*
Fashion F **Van Allan**	488	481	**Laskys** *Hi-fi equipment*
Fashion F **Wallis**	490	483	**Harry Fenton** *Fashion M*
Fashion F **Just Looking**	494	485	**Tax Free Shop** *Fabrics M*
Shoes **Ravel**	498	487	**Alfred Marks** *Employment agency*
Jewellers **Ernest Jones**	500	487	**Cardshop** *Posters & cards*
Shoes **Saxone**	502	489	**Village Gate** *Fashion M*
		491	**Revone** *Fashion F*
		493	**Lord John** *Fashion M*
Portman street			**Park street**
STORE **LITTLEWOODS**	506	499	**Chinacraft**
Fashion M **Lord John**	522	501	**C & A** *STORE*
Fashion F **Dorothy Perkins**	524		
Fashion F **Jax**	526	523	**Jacey Galleries** *Arcade*
Handbags **Salisbury**	528	529	**Marbles** *Fashion market*
Fashion F **Paige**	530	531	**Unit Three** *China & glass*
Shoes **Dolcis**	532	533	**Syndicate** *Fashion & furs MF*
Fashion F **Evans**	538	535	**Jean Machine**
		539	**Quality Inn** *Restaurant*
Old Quebec street			**Park lane**
Marble Arch *Restaurant*	542		
Fashion F M & Camping centre **Milletts**	542		
Oriental Jewel Co	546		
Marble Arch ⊖			
Cumberland Hotel			
Barclays Bank	556		**Marble Arch**
Great Cumberland place			

Bond street — new and old

Left		Right	
			Oxford street
Shoes **Dolcis**	87		**Manfield** *Shoes*
Fashion M **Take Six**	90		
Fashion F **Elle**	92		
Tweeds & knitwear **W. Bill**	93		
Old Vienna Restaurant	94	79	Trumps Nursing Agency
Fashion F **Ronnie Stirling**	94	79	Ivy Gibson *Friendship & Marriage Bureau*
		79	**Fransisco** *Fashions M*
Blenheim street		78	**Elliot** *Shoes*
Shoes **Kurt Geiger**	95		**Dering street**
Fashion F **Place Vendôme**	95	75	**Lothars** *Fashion F*
Royal Bank of Scotland	97	74	**Lucy's** *Fashion F*
Linens **Frette**	98	74	**Alexander Juran** *Oriental carpets*
Employment agency **Manpower**	98	73	**Brook St. Bureau** *Employment agency*
Knitwear **The Bond Street Boutique**	99	73	**Saint Laurent** *Shoes & fashion F M*
Dr Deimel *Underwear*	99	72	**Midas** *Shoes*
Leather **Skincraft**	100	71	**Jones** *Fashion M*
Fashion F **Diane Warren**	101	70	London Girl *Employment agency*
Fashion F **Crocodile**	102	70	**Brasserie** *Restaurant*
Shoes **Ravel**	103	69	**Coronel** *Fashion F*
Travel agency **Milbanke**	104		

Fashion **Daniel Hechter** 105
Office stationers **Ryman** 106
British Airways (Overseas Division) 107
Fashion M **Chavila** 108
Employment agency St Paul's 108
Hairdresser **Stephen Way** 109
Henna Advice Centre 109
Shoes **Russell & Bromley** 109
Handbags **Le Soir** 109

Barclays Bank
Bond Street Gallery 111
Fashion F **Saint Laurent** 113
Shoes **Magli** 114
Employment agency Alfred Marks 115
Shoes **Bally** 116
Jewellers & silversmiths **Crombie** 118
Book Keepers Bureau 118
Employment agency Winfred Johnson 118
Fashion M **Cecil Gee** 122
Samars Carpet Gallery 123
Arcade **Bond Street Antique Centre** 124
Marriage bureau **Heather Jenner** 124
Graus Antiques 125
Fashion M **Herbie Frogg** 125
Cameras **Wallace Heaton** 127
Midland Bank 129

Grosvenor street

Chinacraft 130
Fashion M **Beale & Inman** 131
Fashion F **Fiorucci** 133
Fashion MF **Pierre Balmain** 134
Fashion M **Serge** 135
Cyprus Carpets 137
Silver & goldsmiths **S. J. Phillips** 139
Fashion M **Ascott** 140
Olympic Travel 141
Chemist **Savory & Moore** 143
London Academy of Modelling 143
Antiques **Frank Partridge** 144
Fine art dealers **Wildenstein** 147
Fine Art Society 148
Luggage **Henry's** 149
Fashion & travel **Ireland House** 150

Bruton street

Luxury goods **Hermès** 152
Fashion F **Courrèges** 155
Air France 158
Shirts & knitwear M **A. Sulka** 159
New Churchills Club 160
Barclays Bank 160
Employment agency **Kelly Girl** 161
Shoes M **Churohes** 163
Fashion F **Ted Lapidus** 163

Grafton street

Luxury accessories **Asprey** 165

Fashion **Ch Rowes**
Hair salon **Vidal Sassoon** 171
Fashion F **Ports** 172
Fashion F **Chloé** 173
Fashion F **Robina** 174
Jewellers **Cartier** 175
Shoes M **Henry Maxwell** 177
Jewellers **Chaumet** 178
Jewellers **Kutchinsky** 179
Jewellers **Boucheron** 180
Silver & goldsmiths **Mappin & Webb** 180

Leather goods **Loewe** 25
Travel agency **Inghams** 26
Luxury goods **Gucci** 27
The Royal Arcade 28
Silver & jewellery **Holmes** 29
Model agency Gavin L. B. Robinson 30
Shoes **Bally** 30
Accessories F **Susan** 31
Beauty salon **Yardley** 33

Stafford street

Midland Bank 36

Leather goods **Andrew Soos** 37

Diamond merchants **Charig** 38

Marlborough Fine Art Gallery 39

Lloyds Bank 39
Employment agency Brook Street 41
Persian Carpet Bazaar 41

---

68 **Myers** Office equipment
68 **Susan** Handbags
67 **Just Looking** Fashion F
66 **The Chelsea Cobbler** Shoes
65 **Bently & Co** Jewellers
64 **Dixons** Cameras

Brook street

FENWICKS STORE

55 Bernadette Bureau Employment agency
54 Smythson of Bond Street Leather goods
Keith Prowse Ticket agency
53 Jasons Fabrics
51 The White House Linen
50 Chapell Music Centre
47 Pinet Shoes

Maddox street

46 Khan Carpets
45 Campkins Camera Centre
43 **Régine** Fashion F
42 Stanley Lowe Fabrics
41 Frost & Reed Paintings
40 Mallett & Son Antiques
38 Originelle Fashion F
37 Gerald Austin Fashion M
36 Medway Shoes
34 Sotheby Auctioneer
31 Bond Street Carpets
31 Hubert Fashion M
29 Christina Fashion F
28 Céline Accessories F
27 Castel Fashion F
26 Tessiers Gold & silversmiths
24 **Russell & Bromley** Shoes F M

Conduit street

23 Philip Landau Fashion M
23 Cuero Suede & leather
22 Fior Jewellery
22 Cameo Corner Antiques
21 Indian Tourist Office
20 Elizabeth Arden Beauty salon
18 Aerolineas Argentinas
17 Air India

Clifford street

16 Watches of Switzerland
16 Stephen Peters Fashion M
15 George Jensen Silversmith
14a Piaget Watches
13 Oriental Carpet Galleries
14 Town & Country Fashion F
12 Janet Reger Lingerie
11 Philip Antrobus Jewellers
10 Adèle Davis Fashion F
10a R. W. Yeo Jewellers
9a Booty Jewellers
9 The Platinum Shop Jewellery
8 Trouser House Fashion M
8 John Mitchell Fine paintings
6 Etienne Aigner Fashion M F
5 Rolex Watches
4 Frank T. Sabin Gallery
1 National Westminster Bank

Burlington gardens

24 Feragamo Shoes & accessories
23 Truefitt & Hill Hair salon M
23 Rare Carpet Gallery
19 Juschi Fashion F
18 Bill Gibb Fashion F
17 André Bogaert Jewellers
17 Clough Antiques
16 Kalman Newman Fabrics M
16 Delman Shoes
16 Rayne House Shoes
14 Colnaghi Galleries Paintings
13 Leger Galleries Paintings
13 Benson & Hedges Tobacconist
12 Ghana Airways
11 Brainin Cashmeres
11 Christine Shaw Beauty school
10 Lufthansa German Airlines
9 Argos
9 T. Zubair Carpets
7 Mayfair Carpet gallery
7 Dowmunt Gallery Paintings
6 The Embassy Club

Left side	No.		No.	Right side
Fine Art **Agnew**	43		6	**Hills Cashmere House & Gift Boutique**
Contemporary Art **New Grafton Gallery**	43		5	**Royal Copenhagen Porcelain Co**
Jewellers **Kirby & Bunn**	44		4	**Fenzi** Fashion M
Amber **Sac Freres**	45		3	**Ackerman** Sporting prints
Knitwear **Scots Corner**	46		2	**Goodes** China & glass
Pearl jewellery **Ciro Pearls**	48		1a	F. B. Meyrowitz Optician
Qantas Airways	49		1	**Jean Renet** Jeweller

Piccadilly

Green park ⊖

Regent street

Left side	No.		No.	Right side
Employment agency Alfred Marks	271			*Great Castle street*
Fashion M Dandy	269			
Restaurant & Pizzeria	267			
Restaurant **Old Kentucky**	265			PETER ROBINSON STORE
Underwear **Damart Thermawear**	263			
Oxford street		⊖		*Oxford Circus*
Italian airways Alitalia	251		266	**Wedgwood** Gift shop
Barclays Bank	251		262	**Mates** Fashion M
National Westminster Bank	249		260	**Bally** Shoes
Princes street			256	**Lord John** Fashion M F
Fabrics M & tailor **Dalah & Sons**	247		246	National Westminster Bank
Hearing aid centre **Scrivens Fortiphone**	245			
Cloth specialist **Charles H. White**	243			*Little Argyll street*
Saxone Shoes for Men	241			
Posters & cards **Cardshop**	239			
Stewarts of Scotland	235			
Pub & restaurant Verreys	233			
Fabrics & knitwear **Court of Regent Street**	231			DICKENS & JONES STORE
Fred Olsen Shipping Lines	229			
Bennet Travel Bureau	229			
Hanover street				
Gateway Building Society	227			
Employment agency Drake Personnel	225			
Irish airlines Aer Lingus	223			
Maddox street				*Great Marlborough street*
Posters **Athena**	221			
Employment agency Alfred Marks	219			
British cloth **Tops**	217			
Hair salon F **Robert Fielding**	215			LIBERTY'S STORE
Cyprus Trade & Tourist Centre	213			
Linguaphone Institute	207			
Furs-for-all by Henry Noble	205			
Employment agency Office Overload	205		208	Barclays Bank
K Shoes	203			
Conduit street				*Foubert's place*
Italian Tourist Office	201		204	**Jaeger** Fashion F
Employment agency Reed	197a		200	**Hamleys** Toys
Greek National Tourist Office	195		198	**House of Chinacraft**
Fabrics M **Excellence**	193		188	**Waring & Gillow** Furnishings, etc
The Scotch House	191		186	**Caterpillar** Shoes F
Jeweller **Pravins**	189		184	**Elliott** Shoes
Jeweller **Peter Trevor**	189		182	**Boots** Chemist, gifts, records, etc
Fabrics M **Lords**	187		180	**Richard Shops** Fashion F
Israeli airlines El Al	185		178	**Ciro Pearls** Jewellers
Noble Furs	183		176	**The Scottish Shop**
Regent Textiles	181		174	Royal Air Maroc
Royal Jordanian airways Alia	177		174	Moroccan Tourist Office
Fabrics M **All Woollens Ltd**	175		172	**Krantz** Fashion M
Employment agency Brook Street Bureau	173		170	**Mappin & Webb** Jewellers & luggage
Saudi Arabian Airlines	171		160	**Hepworths** Fashion M
Spanish airlines Iberia	169		158	**Wedgwood Gered** China
			156	**Miss Selfridge** Fashion F
New Burlington street				*Beak street*
Japanese National Tourist Office	167		154	**Lawleys** English china & glass
Fashion M Burberrys	165		152	**Rayne** Shoes
B & I Shipping Line	155		146	**The Needlewoman Shop**
Wine merchants **Hedges & Butler**	153		140	Air Canada
Employment agency Alfred Marks	151		138	**Dalah** Fabrics M
Singapore Airlines	145		134	**Sony Showroom** TV, radio, hi-fi, etc
Yugoslavian National Tourist Office	143		132	Lloyds Bank
Fashion M The Village Gate	141			
China **Wilson & Gill**	137			
Midland Bank	133			
Heddon street				*Regent place*
Fashion M Harry Fenton	131		130	**Carrington** Jewellers
Fashion M Airey & Wheeler	129			
Ferries **Townsend Thoresen**	127		126	Bulgarian National Tourist Office
Cutlery **Clements**	125			
New Gallery Centre	123		124	**T. & J. Perry** Jewellers
Leeds Building Society	121a			
Fabrics M **Fine Textiles**	121		122	**Nu-Swift** Fire Extinguishers
Pencraft	119			

Regent street continued

Left (odd side)		No.	Right (even side)
	Mayfair Coin Co	117	
	Royal Bank of Scotland	113	
		114	**Burton Tailoring** Fashion M
		112	**Garrard** Gold & silversmiths
	Vigo street		
	Glasshouse street		
Fashion M	**Austin Reed**	103	
Shoes	**Peter Lord**	101	
Fabrics M	**Daish**	99	
		100	**Aquascutum** Fashion F M
		90	**Michael Barrie** Fashion M
		88	**Seefeld's Plaza**
	Swallow street		
Fabrics M	**Cloth House Shop**	95	
	Regent Jewellers	93	
Staff consultants	**Challoner Service**	91	
	Shoes **Lotus**	91	
Fashion M	**Acuman**	89	
Jewellery & handbags	**Salisburys**	87	
	Solrae Air Luggage	83	
British Airways (Overseas Division)		75	
	Chinacraft	71	
	Village Bookshop	69	
	British Airways	65	
STORE	**SWAN & EDGAR**		
		84	**The Scotch House** Fashion F M
		82	**K Shoes**
	Quadrant Arcade		
		80	**Collingwood** Jewellers
		78	**Saxone** Shoes
		76	**Lord John Executive** Fashion M
		74a	**Angus Steak House** Restaurant
		74	**Le Relais** Restaurant
		70	**Dandy** Fashion M
		72	Cafe Royal
		68	National Sporting Club
		62	**Huppert Knitwear House**
		56	**Dunn & Co** Fashion M
		54	Regent Shipping Line
		52	Barclays Bank

Piccadilly Circus

Carnaby street

Great Marlborough street

James Galt Toys

Left		No.	Right	No.	
Restaurant	**Chubbies**				
Fashion M	**Lord John**				
Pub	**The Shakespeare's Head**				

Foubert's place

Left		No.	No.	Right	
			31	**Aristos** Fashion F	
			30	**Sir Harry** Fashion M	
			29	**Lady Jane** Fashion F	
			28	**Raj Enterprises** Indian Fashion	
			28a	**Fancy That of London** Souvenirs	
Florist	**René**	32			
Luxury goods	**Rosemary & Thyme**	33			
Souvenirs	**Gear**	35			
Fashion M	**Lord John**	39			
Arcade	**Carnaby Court**				
	Merc Jeans Shop				
Fashion F M	**Flea Market**				

Lowndes court

| 25 | **Chandis** Fashion M F |
| 25 | **Roma of Carnaby** Fashion M F |

Jeans	**Reward**	39
Souvenirs	**Cerex**	40
	Jean Masters	41
Fashion M	**Lord John**	43

Marlborough court

24	**Take 6** Fashion M
23	**Donis** Fashion M
21	**Rock Dreams** Records & jewellery

Ganton street

Left		No.	No.	Right
Shoes M	**Ravel**	44	20	**Superama**
Shoes	**Topper**	44	15	**Rock Dreams** Records & jewellery
	Pop's Shop	46a	14	**Catch** Gifts
Fashion F	**2nd Gear**	46	13	**Daedalus** Jewellery, leathergoods
Fashion M	**Paul's**	47	12	**Go Downtown** Fashion M F
Jewellery & leathergoods	**Daedalus**	47a	11	**Cerex** Souvenirs
Jewellery & gifts	**Phase Two**	48	10	**Shan** Fashion M F
Reggae club	**Columbos**	49	9	**Raj Enterprises** Fashion M F
Fashion F & souvenirs	**Match Point**	49	5	**Pussy Galore** Fashion F
Fashion Ch	**Kids in Gear**	49	5	**Carnaby Super Store**
Jewellery	**The Great Frog**	50	4	**Dayvilles** Ices & hot dogs
Souvenirs	**Lord Kitcheners**	52	3	**Strikes** Restaurant
	Lisa Drugstore	52	2	**Mina** Indian fashions
Indian Fashions	**Mina**	56		
Leatherwear & glass	**Anchorage Arts**	57		

Beak street

Kings road

Sloane square

STORE **PETER JONES**

No.	
⊖	*Sloane square*
27	**Tutto** Fashion F
27a	**Chelsea Jeans**
9	Post Office
11	**ABC Bakeries**
	HoHo Restaurant
13	**Macmarket** Food store
17	**NSS** Newsagents & tobacconists
19	**Victoria Wine**
21	Ladbrokes Turf accountant
23	Brook Street Employment agency
25	**Honey Jeans** Fashion F
25	Search Employment agency
27	**Lisa of Chelsea** Fashion F
29	**Boots** Chemist

Cadogan gardens

Left side (even numbers)

Shoes **Lilley & Skinner**	34
London School of Bridge	34
Fashion F **Sidney Smith**	36
Fashion M **Cecil Gee**	44
Charlie's Wine Bar	46
Hair salon Sissors	46a
Shoes **Chelsea Cobbler**	54
Fashion F M **Jean Machine**	54
Old Kentucky Restaurant	56
Shoes **Russell & Bromley**	64
Shoes **Dolcis**	68

Blacklands terrace

Fashion F M **Lord John**	72

Lincoln street

Restaurant Guys & Dolls	74
Syndicate	76
Restaurant Pizzaland	80
Fashion F M **Mates by Irvine Sellars**	82
Fashion F **Fifth Avenue**	84
Shoes **Sacha International**	86
Fashion F **Just Looking**	88
Fashion F **Girl**	90
Shoes **Bally**	92
Restaurant London Steak House	94
Fashion F **Wallis**	96
Restaurant The Chelsea Kitchen	98
Wines Peter Dominic	100
Fashion F **Wakefords**	102
Fashion M **John Michael**	102

Anderson street

Chelsea Building Society	112
Fashion M **Cassidy**	114

Tryon street

Fashion M **Just Men**	118
Shoes **Elliot**	120
Fashion F **Dorothy Perkins**	
Hair salon **Gallico**	
The Scotch House	
Supermarket **Sainsbury**	
Chemist **Boots**	
Fashion M **Oscars**	122a
American goods **Rock Dreams**	124
Fashion M F **Mates**	124
Restaurant Rumples Diner	126
Shoes **Kickers**	128
Shoes **Ravel**	130
Cheque Point	130
Shoes **Bally**	132

Bywater street

Bakery Beaton's	134
Fashion Anita's	136
Pub Markham Arms	138
Markham Pharmacy	138a

Markham square

Barclays Bank	140
Shoes M **Topper**	146

Markham street

Jubilee place

Lloyds Bank	164
Farha Jeans	168
Fashion F M **The Westerner**	170
Restaurant Choy's	172
Fashion M **Michael Barrie**	174
Fashion F **Miss Chelsea**	176

Burnsall street

Fashion M **Tipo**	178
Fashion M **Cassidy**	180
Records & tapes Les Disques	182a

Right side (odd numbers)

31	**Lady Lisa** Fashion F
31	**My Shop** Hair salon F M
	Duke of York's Headquarters

Cheltenham terrace

33	National Westminster Bank
33a	**Family** Fashion F M
33b	**Joe's** Fashion F
33c	**Don Luigi** Restaurant
33d	**Dandy** Fashion M
33e	**Martins** Radios
33f	**Anschel** Jewellery
	Texaco Petrol station

Walpole street

35	**Safeways** Supermarket

Royal avenue

49	**Harlequin** Arcade store
49	Chelsea Drugstore Disco bar
51	Victoria Sporting & Racing Turf accountant
53	**Dayvilles** Ices
55	**Andrews** Butchers
57	**Revolver** Fashion F
59	**Topper** Shoes & fashion F M

Wellington square

61	**Gee 2** Fashion M
63	**Robert Fielding** Hair salon & wigs
65	**Jean Machine** Fashion F M
67	**Take 6** Fashion M
67a	**J. Wiseman** Furs
69	**Take 6** Fashion M

Smith street

71	**Stanley Adams** Fashion M
75	**Chopra** Fashion M F
79	**Thackerays** Fashion M
	Jean Junction
	Downtown Fashion F
	Great Gear Market Fashion etc
	Serge Fashion M
89	**Second Image** Fashion M F
91	**Lolita** Fashion F
93	**Le Bistingo** Fashion F
95	Marco Polo Restaurant
97	**Squire Shop** Fashion M
	Car park
101	**Hanky Panky** Ch
103	**Carvill** Fashion M
105	**Aisling** Fashion F
107	Wedgies Club
109	**Silver Dollar** Fashion M
109	Christian Science Reading Room
113	**It's a Sell Out** Fashion M F
115	**Jean Centre** Fashion F M

Radnor walk

119	Chelsea Potter Pub & restaurant
121	**The Common Market** Fashion F M
123	Victoria Wine
123a	Kendalls & Sons Builders
125	Jean Machine

Shawfield street

125	**Pinto** Fashion M F
127	**Picasso** Restaurant
129	**Quincy-Jones** Fashion M
131	**Village Gate** Fashion M
135	**Antiquarius** Antiques, fashion, jewellery, etc

Left side		Right side	
Electrical Equipment **Ashby**	184	137	**Antiquarius**
Fashion F **Danys**	186	139	**Antiquarius** Antiques, fashion, jewellery, etc
		141	**Antiquarius**
Dry cleaners **Sketchley**	186a		*Flood street*
Fashion F M **Soldier Blue**	188	145	**Jaegar** Fashion F M
		147	**Depot St Tropez** Fashion M F
Restaurant American Haven	190	151	**Ricci Burns** Hair salon F
The Kings Rd Leathers	192	151	W. M. Jones Opticians
Handbags **Shura**	192	153	Victor's Restaurant
Pub Trafalgar	200	153	**Boy** Fashion M
		155a	CHELSEA METHODIST CHURCH
		157	**The Boot Store**
Odeon Cinema		159	G. Dutton Shoes
Furnishings **Habitat**		161	**Jean Machine** Fashion F M
			Chelsea Manor street
National Westminster Bank	224		
Post Office	232		TOWN HALL
Sydney street			
		183	**Chenil Galleries**
		183	**Heath Bullock** Antique furniture
		187	**Camera Craft**
COUNCIL OFFICES	250	193	**A. E. Gould & Sons** Antiques
		193	The Birds Nest Disco & restaurant
		197	The Six Bells Pub
		199	**Hide Park** Antiques & leather furniture
		201	Chelsea Wash Inn Launderette
		203	**Chelsea** Record Centre
Dovehouse street		205	Pizza Pizza Vino Restaurant
CHELSEA FIRE STATION		207	**Givans** Linen
		209	**Wine & Beer Shop**
Manresa road			*Oakley street*
COLLEGE OF SCIENCE & TECHNOLOGY			*Glebe place*
		219	**Tiger Tiger** Toys
		221	**The Bouzy Rouge** Wine shop & restaurant
		229	**Retro** Antique clothes
		231	**Rider Footwear**
		235	Kings Restaurant
		237	**Chelsea Food Fayre**
		239	**The Body Shop** Fashion F
			Bramerton street
Carlyle square		241	**Meeny's** Fashion
		243	**The 243 Shop** Newsagent & tobacconist
		245	D. Kirkham Greengrocer
		245	**Antique Market**
		247	**Joanna Booth** Antiques
		249	Dominic's Restaurant
		251	S. Borris Delicatessen
		253	**Chelsea Antique Market**
		255	**Jeremy** Antiques
		257	**Green & Stone** Artists' materials
		261	**H. Brown** Food store
		263	**Topaz** Accessories M F
		265	**Ripolin** Do-it-yourself shop
		267	**Isaac Lloyd** Chemist
		269	**David Pettifer** Antiques
		271b	Borshtch 'n' Cheers Restaurant
		275	**David Tron** Antiques
		277	**Designers Guild** Furnishings
			Old Church street
Fashion Ch **Small Wonder**	296	279	Kings Road Theatre
Estate agency Jackson Rose	296a		
Pub Cadogan Arms	298	281	**B&V** Gifts
		283	M. Silver & Sons Jewellers
National Westminster Bank	300	285	Gilbert Parr Paintings
Interior designers Osborne & Little	304	287	Raffles Club
Furnishings **Kipling**	306	289	**Heatherington** Fashion F
Design Direction	308	289	Kings Road Jam Restaurant
Dry cleaners One Hour Martinizing	310		**Joanna's Tent** Fashion F
Removals Ford & Son	310		
Restaurant La Gourmet	312		*Paultons square*
Artist materials **Chelsea Art Store**	314		
Restaurant Kennedy's	316		
Antiques **David Tremayne**	320		
Antiques **R. Wearn & Son**	322		
Picture framing Alfred Hecht	324		
Carpets **Bernadout**	328		
Restaurant Toscanini	330		
Restaurant Le Bistingo	334		
Kings Rd Cellars	336		
S. Bachari Antiques	336	303	**Hooper & Purchase** Antique furniture prints
Restaurant Casserole	338		Bamboo Kitchen Chinese take-away
Fabrics **Liberty Prints**	340a	305	**Chelsea Trading** Furniture
Restaurant Thierry	342	307	**Ciancimino** Furniture antique & modern
Antiques **David Drey**	344	309a	**Portfolio** Artists' prints
Barclays Bank	348	313	**Fruit Fly** Fashion
The Vale			
GLC Ambulance station			

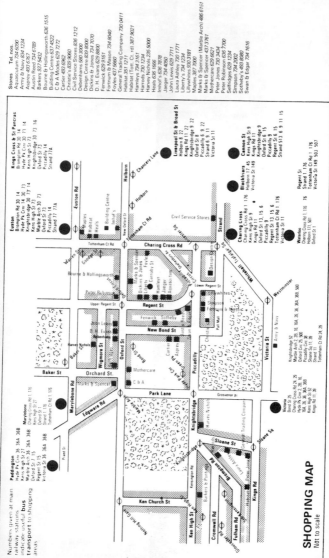

SHOPPING MAP
Not to scale

Conversion charts

Clothing Sizes
*In London you will find both English and American sizing in the
clothes shops, whereas there is a combination of English and
Continental sizing in the shoe shops.*

Dresses

English	10	12	14	16	18	20	
	32	**34**	**36**	**38**	**40**	**42**	**44**
U.S.A.	8	10	12	14	16	18	20
Continental	38	40	42	44	46	48	50

Shoes

English	3	$3\frac{1}{2}$	4	$4\frac{1}{2}$	5	$5\frac{1}{2}$	6	$6\frac{1}{2}$	7	$7\frac{1}{2}$	8
U.S.A.		$4\frac{1}{2}$	5	$5\frac{1}{2}$	6	$6\frac{1}{2}$	7	$7\frac{1}{2}$	8	$8\frac{1}{2}$	9	$9\frac{1}{2}$
Continental		35	36	37	37	38	38	39	40	40	41	41

Hats

English	$6\frac{5}{8}$	$6\frac{3}{4}$	$6\frac{7}{8}$	7	$7\frac{1}{8}$	$7\frac{1}{4}$	$7\frac{3}{8}$	$7\frac{1}{2}$	$7\frac{5}{8}$
U.S.A.		$6\frac{3}{4}$	$6\frac{7}{8}$	7	$7\frac{1}{8}$	$7\frac{1}{4}$	$7\frac{3}{8}$	$7\frac{1}{2}$	
Continental		54	55	56	57	58	59	60	61	62

Glove sizes are international.

Weights & Measures

Feet/Metres

English ·	1	2	3	4	5	6	7	8	9	10
Continental	0.3	0.6	0.9	1.2	1.5	1.8	2.1	2.4	2.7	3.0

Pounds/Kilograms

English	1	2	3	4	5	6	7	8	9	10
Continental	0.4	0.9	1.4	1.8	2.3	2.7	3.2	3.6	4.1	4.5

Pints/Litres

English	$\frac{1}{4}$		$\frac{3}{4}$	1	2	3	4	5
Continental	0.1	0.3	0.4	0.6	1.1	1.7	2.3	2.8

GETTING OUT

Airports

Both the airports servicing London are quite a distance outside the city. If you wish to reach them by car you will find ample parking facilities for both brief and long periods, but the easiest way of getting to Heathrow is by the special buses which go from the Air Terminals (see below) and to Gatwick by train from Victoria Station. Both airports are amply provided with shops, banks, and other necessary facilities for passengers.

Gatwick Airport
Horley, Surrey. Tel Crawley 28822.
London Airport (Heathrow)
Bath Rd, Heathrow, Middx. 01-759 4321.

Air terminals

British Airways
Victoria Air Terminal, Buckingham Palace Rd SW1. 01-834 2323. Reservations 01-828 9711. British Airways Overseas Division, most inter-continental and world airlines. *OPEN 24 hrs.*
Air Lingus
Tara Hotel, Wright's Lane, Kensington High St W8. 01-734 1212.
Pan American Air Terminal
Semley Place SW1. 01-759 2595. Pan Am flights, National & Malaysian Airlines. Coaches for Varig and Qantas, to and from Heathrow. *OPEN 06.45-18.30.*
TWA Town Terminal
380 Kensington High St W8. 01-602 0141. Flights only. Coaches to and from Heathrow. *OPEN 07.00-15.30.*
British Caledonian
Central London Air Terminal, Victoria Station SW1. 01-834 9411. Departures only. To West Africa & South America. *OPEN 24 hrs.*
West London
Cromwell Rd SW7. 01-370 5411. British Airways European Division, operating coaches to London (Heathrow) Airport. *OPEN 06.00-22.30.*

Rail terminals

British Rail Travel Centre
12 Lower Regent St SW1. Personal callers only.
Booking centre for rail travel in Britain and rail and sea
journeys to the Continent and Ireland. Several
languages spoken. See also under 'Information
centres'.
Charing Cross *(South)*
Strand WC2. Information 01-928 5100.
Euston *(North)*
Euston Rd NW1. Information 01-387 7070.
King's Cross *(North)*
Euston Rd N1. Information 01-837 3355.
Liverpool Street *(East & Continental)*
Liverpool St EC2. Information 01-283 7171. Continental
01-247 9812. Car bookings 01-623 1831.
Paddington *(West)*
Praed St W2. Information 01-262 6767.
Victoria *(South & Continent)*
Terminus Place, Victoria St SW1. Information 01-928
5100. Continental 01-834 2345. Car ferry 01-730 3440.
Waterloo *(South)*
York Rd SE1. Information 01-928 5100.

Buses and coaches

Green Line Coaches
Enquiries Reigate 42411.
Operate a regular service to approx 30 miles from
London. The main picking up points are at Baker St,
Buckingham Palace Rd, Eccleston Bridge and the
Minories Coach station.
London Transport buses
Enquiries: 01-222 1234.
Free maps of all London bus routes from underground
station ticket offices.
Other information and LT publications from

Coach stations

Kings Cross Coach Station
National Travel, 250 Pentonville Rd N1. 01-278 7081.
Coach services to East Anglia, Southend and Stansted
airports.
Victoria Coach Station
164 Buckingham Palace Rd SW1. 01-730 0202. The
main provincial coach companies operate from here,
travelling all over Britain and Continent. Booking
necessary.

Day trips from London

Cheap day excursion and special country afternoon tickets are available to most places by rail. Buses and coaches leave regularly from Victoria Coach Station. EC = early closing day.

Blenheim Palace

Woodstock, Oxfordshire. Woodstock 811325. A great classical style ducal palace by Sir John Vanbrugh 1705-22. The estate was given by Queen Anne to John Churchill, Duke of Marlborough for his victory over Louis XIV at Blenheim in 1704. Winston Churchill was born here. Fine paintings, tapestries and furniture. The park was landscaped first by Wise and later by Capability Brown in 1760, who dammed the small stream to create two great lakes, keeping Vanbrugh's original bridge, and forming a dam ingeniously separating the two levels of water. London 60 miles (A34). *OPEN Mar-Oct 11.30-17.00 daily. Admission charge.*

Brighton, Sussex

Known as 'Little London by the sea', this once poor fishing village has been a lively, bustling seaside resort ever since the Prince Regent set up his court in the fabulous oriental-domed Pavillion. Fashionable shops, splended Regency terraces, good pubs and restaurants, cockle stalls, fairs and sport of all kinds. 5 miles of beach and two magical Victorian piers. Train 1 hr. *EC Wed or Thur.* London 48 miles.

Cambridge

A great university of spires, mellow colleges and riverside meadows, bordering the Cam. The famous 'Backs' and the lovely bridges are best seen by hiring a punt. The 20 or so colleges are from the 13th cent onwards including Trinity by Wren, Kings by James

Gibbs and the modern Queens by Basil Spence. The city also contains the superb Fitzwilliam Museum, the notable Botanic Garden and some very fine churches. Train 1½ hrs. *EC Thur.* London 55 miles (A 10).

Canterbury, Kent
Pleasant old walled city on the River Stour, dominated by the magnificent Gothic cathedral, containing the shrine of Thomas à Becket (murdered 1170) and the tomb of the Black Prince. Good local museum in West Gate. Train 1½ hrs. *EC Thur.* London 56 miles (M2).

Chichester, Sussex
An old Roman city walled by the Saxons and graced by its beautiful 12th cent cathedral. Now mostly Georgian in character. Fine 16th cent Butter Cross, a medieval Guildhall and modern Festival Theatre, built 1962. Excellent harbour for sailing. Train 1½ hrs. *EC Thur.* London 63 miles.

Ham House
Petersham, Surrey. 01-940 1950. Superb 17th cent country house built on an 'H' plan. Lavish Restoration interior. Important collection of Stuart furniture. *OPEN Apr-Sept 14.00-18.00 Tues-Sun & B. Hols; Oct-Mar 12.00-16.00 Tues-Sun. CLOSED New Year's, G. Fri, Xmas, Box. Small admission charge.*

Hampton Court Palace
Hampton Court, Middx. 01-977 8441. Royal palace built 1514 for Cardinal Wolsey with later additions by Henry VIII and Wren. Sumptuous state rooms painted by Vanbrugh, Verrio and Thornhill. Famous picture gallery of Italian masterpieces. Orangery, mellow courtyards, the 'great vine' and the maze. The formal gardens are probably among the greatest in the world. Exotic plants from 16th cent. (The Mitre opposite). *OPEN 09.30-17.30 Mon-Sat, 11.00-17.30 Sun; Mar, Apr & Oct closes 16.30 Mon-Sat, 14.00-16.30 Sun; Nov-Feb closes 15.30, 14.00-15.30 Sun. CLOSED G. Fri, Xmas, Box. Admission charge.*

Hatfield

Hatfield, Hertfordshire. Hatfield 62823. A mellow and completely preserved Jacobean mansion with magnificent interior built in 1607-11 by Robert Cecil, 1st Earl of Salisbury and still the home of the Cecil family. The Tudor Old Royal Palace nearby was the home of Queen Elizabeth I. Collection of 16th-, 17th- and 18th cent portraits, manuscripts and relics. London 20 miles (A1). *House OPEN 25th Mar-7th Oct 12.00-17.30 Tues-Sat & B. Hols, 14.00-17.30 Sun. CLOSED G. Fri. Admission charge.*

Marble Hill House

Richmond Rd, Twickenham, Middx. 01-892 5115. Palladian-style house built in 1728 by Roger Morris, with interior and furnishings in period. Summer exhibition of paintings. *OPEN 10.00-17.00 every day except Fri. CLOSED G.Fri & Xmas. Free.*

Osterley Park House

Thornbury Rd, Osterley, Middx. 01-560 3918. Remodelled by Robert Adam 1761-78 on an already fine Elizabethan building built round a courtyard. The magnificent interiors with furniture, mirrors, carpets and tapestry all show the elegance and richness of Adam's genius. *OPEN Apr-Sept 14.00-18.00, Oct-Mar 12.00-16.00. Admission in morning by special arrangement. CLOSED Mon (except B. Hols), Xmas Eve, Xmas, Box, New Year's, G. Fri. Free. Park OPEN all year 10.00-dusk.*

Oxford

A university city of spires and fine college buildings on the Thames and the Cherwell and dating from the 13th cent. The Sheldonian Theatre by Wren, the Radcliffe Camera by Gibbs and the 15th cent Bodleian Library are particularly notable. Visit also the famous old Botanic Garden and the Ashmolean Museum. Train 1½ hrs. *EC Thur.* London 65 miles.

Sissinghurst Castle

Sissinghurst, Kent, Sissinghurst 250. The soft red-brick remains of the walls and buildings of a once extensive Tudor manor, enchantingly transformed by the late Victoria Sackville-West and Sir Harold Nicolson into numerous enclosed walled gardens. Each is different in character and outstandingly beautiful in its richness of flowers and shrubs. London 40 miles (A21). *OPEN 1st April-15th Oct 12.00-18.30 Mon-Fri, 10.00-18.30 weekends & B. Hols. Admission charge. No dogs.*

Stratford-on-Avon

The birthplace of William Shakespeare (1564-1616). The town is still Elizabethan in atmosphere with overhung gables and timbered inns. Visit the poet's birthplace in Henley St, his house at New Place, Anne Hathaway's cottage and the museum and picture gallery. Train 2½ hrs. *EC Thur.* London 90 miles.

Winchester, Hants

The ancient Saxon capital of England set among lovely rolling chalk downland. The massive, square towered Norman cathedral, with its superb vaulted Gothic nave, contains the graves of King Canute, Izaac Walton and Jane Austen. The 'round table of King Arthur' is in the remains of the Norman castle. Train 1½ hrs. *EC Thur.* London 65 miles (A30).

Windsor Castle

Windsor, Berks. Windsor 63106. An imposing 800-year-old medieval fortress. 12th cent Round Tower built by Henry II. St George's chapel is fine 16th cent perpendicular. Magnificent state apartments. *OPEN Jan-mid March 10.30-15.00; mid Mar-mid Oct 10.30-17.00 (Sun from 13.00); mid Oct-Dec 10.30-15.00. CLOSED Sun, mid Oct-mid Mar and when the Queen is in residence — usually 6 weeks at Easter, 3 weeks in Jun and 3 weeks at Xmas. Admission charge.*

Woburn Abbey

Woburn, Bedfordshire. Woburn 666. The Duke of Bedford's 18th cent mansion, set in a fine 3,000-acre park landscaped by Humphrey Repton (part of which has been converted into a Safari Park). The house retains the quadrangular plan of the medieval monastery from which it also derived its site and name. Remodelling has occurred at different periods; the west front and the magnificent state apartments were done in 1747-60 by Henry Flitcroft; the south side, the lovely Chinese dairy and the orangery in 1802 by Henry Holland. Incomparable collection of pictures by Rembrandt, Van Dyck, Reynolds, Gainsborough, Holbein and a famous group of fine Canalettos. English and French furniture, porcelain and silver. London 40 miles (M1). *Abbey and Park OPEN Mar 22-Aug 31 10.30-17.00 Mon-Sat, 10.00-17.30 Sun; Sept 1-Oct 24 11.00-16.30 Mon-Sat, 11.00-17.00 Sun, Oct 25-Mar 20 11.00-15.30 daily. Safari Park OPEN 10.00-17.30 weekdays, 10.00-18.00 weekends or until dusk in winter. Admission charge.*

Information centres

These are the main sources of information available to the tourist about events, places or travel.

British Rail Travel Centre

4 Lower Regent St SW1. Personal callers only. British Rail's shop window in the West End. Booking centre for rail travel in Britain and rail-and-sea journeys to the Continent and Ireland. Several languages spoken. Smaller offices at: 14 Kingsgate Parade. Victoria St SW1, 407 Oxford St W1, 170b Strand WC2, 87 King William St EC4.

Travel Enquiry Offices

London Transport offices for enquiries on travel (underground and buses) and general tourist information. Their booklet 'How to get there' (5p) is essential. Also free maps of underground and buses.

St James's Park Underground Station
01-222 1234. *24-hr telephone service.*
Oxford Circus Underground Station
Victoria Station Underground Station
Euston Station Underground Station
King's Cross Underground Station
Piccadilly Circus Underground Station
All OPEN daily 08.00-18.00.

British Tourist Authority

64 St James's St SW1. 01-629 9191. Tourist information about Britain. Nine languages spoken. Literature, some free, some on sale. *OPEN Apr-Oct 09.00-18.00 Mon-Fri, 09.00-14.30 Sat. Nov-Mar 09.00-17.30 Mon-Fri, 09.00-12.30 Sat. CLOSED Sun.*

City of London Information Centre

St Paul's Churchyard EC4. 01-606 3030. Information and advice with specific reference to the 'Square Mile'. Free literature. Essential to get monthly 'Diary of Events' which lists a big choice of free entertainment in the City. *OPEN 09.30-17.00 Mon-Fri, 10.00-16.00 Sat (until 12.30 in winter). CLOSED Sun.*

International Traveller's Aid

Head Office, YWCA, 16 Great Russell St WC1. 01-580 0478. To help any traveller in distress but particularly concerned with young people and mothers travelling with young children. Will meet and escort a traveller across London, but book in advance.

London Tourist Board Information Bureau

Give travel and tourist information. Also information on accommodation. Most languages spoken.

26 Grosvenor Gardens SW1. 01-730 0791.
OPEN summer 09.00-20.00, winter 09.00-18.00.

London tours

By coach

All coach tours start from the addresses given. Commentary given en route. Sightseeing tours to all the main tourist attractions, including Changing the Guard, Westminster Abbey, The City, St Paul's, Windsor Castle and Hampton Court. Also 'London by night'. There is a 24 hour service for travel enquiries: 01-222 1234.

American Express
6 Haymarket SW1. 01-930 4411.

Thomas Cook
45 Berkeley St W1. 01-491 7434.

Evan Evans
Metropolis House, 41 Tottenham Court Rd W1. 01-637 4171.

Frames
25 Tavistock place WC1. 01-387 3488

London Transport Tours
Victoria Coach Station SW1. 01-730 0202. Sightseeing tour *daily every hour* from Grosvenor Gdns and Eros, Piccadilly. Bright red open-topped buses are used. Covers 20 miles of the City and West End.

Red Rover Ticket
A day's unlimited travel on London's red buses for 50p adults, 25p children *weekdays after 09.30, Sat. Sun. B. Hol. any hour.* Available from travel enquiry offices, underground stations and garages.

By private guides

Autoguide
93 Knightsbridge SW1. 01-235 0806. Any sort of tour arranged, from a 1-hr shopping trip to a continental jaunt. Most European languages spoken.

Guides of Britain
71 Burlington Arcade W1. 01-493 3416. Guides to take you on an individual shopping tour. £9.00 per half day with car. Also chauffeur-driven guided tours throughout England — individually tailored.

Horse-drawn carriage tours of residential London
42 Kenning Place Mews. 01-584 7387. A pageant of English social history in London's only private carriage. Visit places you would otherwise never know were there. 1½ hrs from *09.00-12.00. £6.00 per person.*

By foot

Off-beat Tours of London
66 St Michaels St W2. 01-262 9572. Small parties of people conducted by competent guide-lecturers on a gentle 1½ hr walk to unusual and out of the way parts of London. Many different walks. *Each tour 50p adults, 30p children.*

London Walks
20 Alexandra Rd N8. 01-889 7288. Meet at various underground stations for topical walks through London. *Weekdays May-Oct.* Topics include Dickens' London, Jack the Ripper, Ghosts of the West End. *Walks 1½-2 hrs. Students ½ price. Children free.*

Self drive car hire

Price depends on season and size of car, plus mileage.
Avis Rent-a-Car
35 Headfort Place SW1. 01-245 9862. *07.00-22.00.*

Also Thurloe Place, Cromwell Rd SW7.
01-581 2252. *08.00-18.00.*
68 North Row W1. 01-629 7811.
OPEN 07.00-20.00.
28-32 Wellington Rd NW8. 01-722 3464. *OPEN 08.30-18.00 Mon-Fri, 08.30-14.00 Sat.*
World-wide reservations at Trident House, Station Rd, Hayes, Middx. 01-848 8733.

Godfrey Davis
Davis House; Wilton Rd SW1. 01-834 8484. *24-hr service.* Rental stations throughout GB.

Hertz, Rent a Car
35 Edgware Rd W2. Daimlers particularly. Self or chauffeur driven. Stations throughout GB and Continent.

Chauffeur drive

Patrick Barthropp
1 Dorset Mews, Wilton St SW1. 01-245 9171. Rolls-Royce Phantoms and Silver Clouds with liveried chauffeurs, cocktails, TV and stereo. *OPEN 07.30-23.00.*

Hanover Car Hire
6 Wigmore Place, Wigmore St W1. 01-580 0505. A fleet of chauffeur-driven limousines and saloons. *OPEN 08.00-19.00 Mon-Sat.*

INFORMATION

Hotel booking agents

Hotac
80 Wigmore St W1. 01-935 2555. Bookings from London are free. Also take advanced bookings from provinces. *OPEN 09.30-18.00 Mon-Fri.*

Hotel Bookings International
Globegate House, Pound Lane NW10. 01-459 1212. All types of hotel reservations mainly in London. Theatres, coaches, conference rooms booked if required. Reception offices at Gatwick and Heathrow. No charge.

Hotel Booking Service
137 Regent St W1. 01-437 5052. Excellent and knowledgeable service to business firms. *OPEN Mon-Fri 09.30-17.30. Sat 09.30-13.00.*

Hotel Guide
Faraday House, 8-10 Charing Cross Rd WC2. 01-240 3288. First class hotel accommodation service. No charge.

Accommodation Service of the London Tourist Board
4 Grosvenor Gardens SW1. 01-730 9845. Free. Budget accommodation. *OPEN 09.00-22.00 mid June-mid Oct.*

Expotel Hotel Reservations
Dial 01-568 8765 for immediately confirmed hotel reservations. A new computerised system which covers the whole of Great Britain. No charge.

Tipping

Should be an expression of one's pleasure for service rendered, never a duty. Some restaurants automatically add a service charge to the bill — so beware of inadvertently tipping twice. These are suggestions only, there is no rule.

Restaurants 10p in the £1.00. More if you are pleased with the service.
Taxis 5p for a 30p fare — rest in proportion.
Women's hairdressers 15p in the £1.00.

Men's hairdressers 15p in the £1.00.
Cloakroom attendants 5p to 10p per article when you collect.
Washroom services If clean towels provided and individual attention is given 5p.
Commissionaires For getting a taxi 5p to 10p depending on the effort expended.
Inns & Pubs Never at the bar. 5p in the £1.00 for waiter service in the lounge.
Hotels Tip individuals for special service. The rest is on your bill anyway — up to 15%.

Telephone information

Emergency calls 999

Directory enquiries
Great Britain 192
London 142

International calls
You can now dial direct to many European countries, Canada and the USA. If the exchange you want is not listed in the GPO Dialing instructions booklet, ask the operator to put you through to the relevant International Exchange operator.

Telegrams
Inland, Ships & Enquiries 190
International 557
International enquiries 559

Ships telephone service
For telephone calls to ships 100

Radiophone service 141
Financial Times share index & Business News summary 246 8026. Updated four times *daily*.
Time: speaking clock 123
Daily events in and around London
Teletourist in English 246 8041
in French 246 8043
in German 246 8045
in Spanish 246 8047
in Italian 246 8049
Weather forecasts
London area 246 8091
Essex coast 246 8096
Sussex coast 246 8097
Kent coast 246 8098

Passports

Passport Office
Clive House, Petty France SW1. 01-222 8010. *OPEN Mon-Fri 09.00-16.30. Emergencies Mon-Fri 16.30-18.30. Sat, Sun & Public Hols 10.00-12.00. CLOSED Xmas.*

Immigration Office
Lunar House, Wellesley Rd Croydon Surrey. 01-686 0688. Deals with questions concerning the granting of British visas to foreigners and entry under the Commonwealth Immigration Act. Subject to approval, visas are then supplied by the

Foreign Office
Clive House Petty France SW1. 01-930 2323.

Tourist offices

Britain
British Travel, Queen's House, 64 St James's St SW1. 01-629 9191.

Ireland
Irish Tourist Office, Ireland House, 150 New Bond St W1. 01-493 3201.

Jersey
Jersey Tourist Information Office, 118 Grand Buildings, Trafalgar Square WC2. 01-930 1619.

Northern Ireland
Northern Ireland Tourist Board, 11 Berkeley St W1. 01-493 0601.

Scotland
Scottish Tourist Board, 5 Pall Mall East SW1. 01-930 3068.

Foreign exchange facilities

The principal clearing banks and their branches throughout London are always very willing to help overseas visitors. Some banks have special travel departments. Travellers cheques may be exchanged at any time during normal banking hours: *09.30-15.30 Mon-Fri.*

Many of the principal London hotels operate their own foreign exchange facilities for the convenience of their guests. The rates of commission are generally a little higher than that of banks.

Chequepoint Services are open seven days a week until midnight. They serve an obvious need outside banking hours. Commission rates vary. Branches on Gloucester Rd, King's Rd, Queensway, Earl's Court Rd and Old Brompton Rd.

Emergencies

Accident
Most large general hospitals have a casualty department but they are not always open 24 hrs. In an emergency or accident, wherever you are, dial 999. The operator will give you the name of the nearest hospital casualty department open at that time and probably arrange an ambulance if necessary.

Cars
The following give a 24-hr breakdown, repair, vehicle recovery and roadside repair service, 7 days a week. All makes of vehicle.

Belsize Garage
27 Belsize Lane NW3. 01-435 5472.
Cavendish Motors
Cavendish Rd NW6. 01-459 0046.
Kensington Park Garage
53 Kensington Pk Rd W11. 01-229 3006.
Parkgate Service Station
15 Parkgate Rd SW11. 01-223 1962. Also petrol.

Chemist
Bliss Chemist
54 Willesden Lane NW6. 01-624 8000.
Boots
Piccadilly Circus W1. 01-930 4761.
Both are open 24 hrs.

Food 24 hours
Canton
11 Newport Place WC2. 01-437 8935. *OPEN 24 hrs.*
Cavendish Hotel
Jermyn St SW1. 01-930 2111. Restaurant *OPEN 24 hrs.*
Empire Grill
85 Gloucester Rd SW7. 01-370 4404. *OPEN 24 hrs.*
Kentucky Fried Chicken
Most of these take-aways are open to 24.00 or later. The following are open 24 hrs.
71 Gloucester Rd SW7
95 Westbourne Grove W2.
245 Kilburn High Rd NW6
Londonderry House Hotel
The Pelican, Old Park Lane W1. 01-493 7292. *OPEN 24 hrs.*

Nicholson's Guides and Maps

LONDON GUIDES

Nicholson's London Guide
Pocket sized, packed full of information, plus many coloured maps.

Nicholson's Student's London
Pocket sized, directed specifically to the student's own needs. Maps and index.

Nicholson's Visitor's London
Specially for the tourist. Full colour picture maps and index.

Nicholson's London Restaurants
London's best restaurants, including cheap meals and pub lunches. Coloured maps.

Nicholson's London Nightlife
Not only the hot spots, but a practical guide to London after dark. Coloured maps.

Nicholson's American's Guide to London
Written by Americans for Americans in the famous Nicholson format. Coloured centre maps.

Nicholson's Guide to Children's London for Parents
All a parent needs to know to keep the kids happy and informed. Coloured centre maps.

LONDON MAPS

Nicholson's Central London Map and Index
30 square miles of central London in two colours and showing one-way streets.

Nicholson's London Street Finder
The famous and long established best seller. Two colours throughout, with large scale centre section showing one-way streets.

Nicholson's Large Street Finder
Large scale and two colour maps throughout for extra legibility.

Nicholson's Hard Back Street Finder
The handy, legible Street Finder for office or car. Two colour maps throughout.

Nicholson's Sightseer's London
An easy guide to localities wherever you are in London.

Nicholson's London Map
Large scale central London with index.

Nicholson's 2 London Maps
Central London map with index plus London route planning map.

Nicholson's Visitor's London Map
Handy full colour fold out map with main sights in 3D.

GREAT BRITAIN GUIDES & MAPS

Nicholson's Great Britain
An easy reference guide to all the family's interests and activities. Fully illustrated and with coloured relief maps.

Nicholson's Waterway's Guides
Five regional guides to the canals of England and Wales with detailed maps.

Nicholson's Real Ale Guide to the Waterways.
Over 1000 pubs on or near the waterways. Maps.

Nicholson's Great Britain Touring Map
Full colour map of Great Britain showing motorways and main roads.